GLOBAL FOOD REVOLUTION!

"Helping Humanity Through The 21ˢᵗ Century Global Food Crisis"

By: Dr. Daniel Daves

Author, Dr. Daniel Daves is available on a limited basis to speak at your event in person or through online media conferencing. He travels in person on location and also uses live streaming education from his office, studio or live from the farm to various groups and audiences. If you are interested in him attending your event, please contact him directly at:

info@globalfoodproviders.com or write:

Dr. Daniel Daves, P.O. Box 179, Mansfield, TX 76063.

You can also connect with him on WhatsApp: +507-6121-0591 or on Facebook. Check out Facebook "Global Food Providers" for prototype farm updates.

Our prototype farm offers group tours and educational classes on a limited basic on our prototype farm in Rovira Abajo, Chiriqui, Panama. (www.globalfoodproviders.com)

Global Food Providers is a subsidiary of Children's Feeding Network, Inc., a U.S. nonprofit 501(c)3 organization. (www.childrensfeedingnetwork.org)

Leadership companion guide available: "Food Is Power" *(pictured above) ISBN:* 978-0-9895919-4-2

Special Thanks:

*Special thanks to Dr. Don Matison who put the original vision into me as he told me when I was a young man, "Food is power. And whoever has the food has the power".

**Special thanks to all who have supported and grown the Global Food Revolution through the years as we searched, moved into location and built the prototype!

***Special thanks also to Milli Myers as well as Ralph & Joyce Poupart for your powerful proofing capabilities!

Mighty Eagle Publishing - www.mightyeagle.com
Paperback, Kindle, PDF, Spanish, Hindi, other languages available or coming soon.

"Global Food Revolution" Paperback ISBN: 978-0-9895919-3-5

"Global Food Revolution" Kindle ISBN: 978-0-9895919-7-3

"It's time that we all re-think how we grow, distribute, package, preserve, purchase and consume our food in the 21st century. That means Global Food Revolution!"

- Dr. Daniel Daves

Author's Primary Note:

The data is overwhelming. The facts are clear. Mankind is headed straight off the cliff of a catastrophic food crisis that will be deeply felt by most every human on planet Earth. It is possible to minimize the collapse, but for that to happen, we must all do our part by making decisive changes and promoting the Global Food Revolution now. Waiting until later will be too late.

Nobility always triumphs over necessity. If we act now out of our nobility, we can help save much of the world from undue pain, suffering and death. But if we wait until we must change out of necessity, then countless lives could be lost. Our necessity will be their calamity.

There is a generation arising who feel deep down that we are not getting the essential nutritional qualities from our foods. This generation also believes that there is no place for systemic corruption, chemical poisoning of our food supplies and unnecessary stripping of natural resources. All at the expense of human health for profits sake? Not on our watch! Our generation is willing to commit a good portion of our lives into food security for our families and communities. We are investing in a radically new nutritional food revolution along with social responsibility and action.

On another note, systemic corporate greed, corruption and unsustainable farming methods could soon fail in such a way that would send many parts of the world into mass famine, despair and death. There is a new generation that is saying, 'No more!" and is demanding a total return to sanity and food security.

Are you one of these who are willing to be a part of this new generation? If so, join us in the Global Food Revolution!

Author's Note About Organic:

While I would love to dive headlong into the subject of organic, near organic or commercial food growing, row planting, cover crops, no till planting, permaculture and more, those are other books for the future. The subject material, education and time to learn organic growing methods will require a lot of commitment and years of study. Patience is required. It is my opinion that most commercial growing systems are not truly sustainable and will eventually collapse. But the efforts to evolve from non-sustainable to sustainable systems will require a full "revolution". We will discuss "revolution" as a concept at the heart and center of this book, which also considers the principles of sustainable and organic farming.

I work with and among people who are located in 3rd world starvation areas. In this Global Food Revolution, I help many people start in their new found agricultural experience. When rushing to feed people who are malnourished or dying, I am not concerned whether the food is fully or partially organic. I want to make sure that the crops yield a harvest so the people can eat. Once we get a controlled harvest, then we can start moving towards sustained organic production.

Don't get me wrong. I love and believe in organics. But I also know that it takes time to learn true organic methods, from the foundational principles to actual application on your farm or in your garden. And when a new person is responsible for a huge upcoming harvest, and if an enemy (fungus, insect, bacteria, virus, etc.) comes to destroy that harvest, do what you must to preserve that harvest from your educational capacity, and learn as you go.

I have a naturopathic doctor friend who has awesome answers for seemingly every health problem. I love his principles for health and I love his saying, *"If you have a physical emergency, get to the hospital emergency room. Stop the bleeding. Get yourself out of critical trouble and get stabilized. Then let's work on a natural way to get you cured."*

I believe that this principle is perfect for growing food. Get going and get your harvest coming. Then let's work on perfecting your program for the greatest, most organic method possible. Use whatever education you have today, and let's build on it moving forward.

Case in point: Our rabbit tea organics program took nine months to get up and running. Our composting program took over a year to figure out. Learning to mix organic fertilizers has taken years of trial and error. Meanwhile we have 18,000 plants on our prototype farm to oversee, maintain and bring to harvest. Patience and education always proves best. Plants grow slow and typically respond to various inputs slower than we desire. True agriculture education takes time.

If your community is starving to death or has experienced agricultural destruction, you are in an emergency room situation. You must plant "super foods, super-fast", and use whatever land, fertilizers and controls you can find. You need to make it happen NOW. *(We actually have these situations in various places around the world all the time. Think "Bahamas hurricane destruction in 2019".)* To force pure organics on newly deputized

7

emergency farmers would be to destroy their needed harvest. They don't know the dynamics yet or how to meet common enemies with true organics. They need calories, fiber and nutrition, and they need it NOW. Once they're out of the emergency room, they can learn organics and the best sustainable way to grow.

I wish you great success. Get started growing with what you know and learn as you go forward.

Key Points:

- *An imminent, catastrophic, food crisis will impact virtually every human being on earth.*
- *To minimize the collapse of food systems, we must do our part as individuals, to promote the Global Food Revolution worldwide.*

"There's enough on this planet for everyone's needs but not for everyone's greed." Mohatmas Gandhi. (And to add to this statement, "Greed is never satisfied." - Tracy Daves)

TABLE OF CONTENTS

Introduction

Do you hear the sound? World hunger and poverty are coming at humanity like a speeding freight train. Global populations are exploding and food production is in decline. While millions around the world are already starving to death annually, the data suggests that the numbers of people who will be starving in the future will multiply at staggering levels.

When nations run out of food and fresh water, they go to war. Many future conflicts are due to arise and many innocent people will die if something is not done about our rising global food crisis. But what can be done to alleviate the critical food shortages that are coming to our world? We need a Global Food Revolution, and we need it now!

Your involvement will make a difference regardless of who you are. From the single college student living in a small apartment on campus to the green thumb gardener who loves to grow delicious foods in his back yard. From an employee who has influence with others on the job, to the owners of a company within the food industry. From the commercial farmer to the billionaire investor. From the high school student to the retired professional or house wife. We all can play a part in the Global Food Revolution which has the capacity to turn the tide of food shortages, mass starvation and international war conflicts. For the sake of humanity, we can secure fresh food, clean water and sustainable natural resources as a model for living in the 21st century and beyond.

This book is about you. It's about activating your passion and creativity to make a change for the good in your world. It's about your involvement in a global movement that will forever change the way that you and your neighbors grow, transport, preserve and consume food. It's about impact, first on a private and personal level, and then on to community, national and global levels.

This book is about empowering you to develop new and innovative ways to provide nutritious food, along with preparation and distribution to your family, community and neighborhood. It's about you developing community help programs or fully profitable business models to promote the growth and distribution of clean, nutritious and organic level foods. It's about sustainable food security for everyone in your relationship circle and realm of desired influence.

This book is about educating your family members and friends about the most basic and wonderful opportunity in the world, learning to grow your own healthy, nutritious and organic level foods for the dinner table.

I will show you how to change your life, health and family through food education and growing techniques. You can then take your personal life education to your community, your city, your nation and to the ends of the earth. Your passion will affect the big picture. Your life and education will speak to people in high places. Your passion will be seen and heard by educators, politicians, princes and kings. You along with others, will help turn the tide of hunger and starvation and you will bring a new level of health and nutrition to the world around you. You will be a world changer, and a global food provider!

I will also address a growing problem between governments, corporations and farmers. Many government agencies are using their power, influence, and sometimes payoffs to squash the small farmer/grower. Their goal is to give more capacity to big agricultural corporations who have a huge advantage over the small grower. This problem must be addressed with revived community support for small producer farms as part of the global food revolution.

Don't get me wrong. There is a huge place for corporate farming and even government agencies and protections. But when government agents use their authority to strip and destroy their own small farmer for personal greed, power, and political influence, these people must be exposed. We must demand that they cease and desist their treasonous harm and destruction of the small, local farmer, and return to true food security for the people.

We must also identify which growing systems are sustainable and which are not. Unfortunately, almost ALL of todays' commercial old school food growing systems are not sustainable for the long term. They will eventually break, leaving a very hungry world full of malnutrition.

I will attempt to show you the current and upcoming food crisis according to global government statistics and reports. I will show you alternatives that you can take right now to make a difference, save (and possibly make) money, and how to set a personal trajectory to change your world. We will discuss: apartment and home gardening, large scale commercial farming, advanced technologies to explode your harvest capacity, and how to set a plan in place to actively change people's lives with your efforts. I will show you how to help those in other parts of the world who will otherwise starve to death or suffer in mass famine. Together, we will build an army of global food educators and providers.

Let's get started today. Prepare to change the world! Raise your right hand and say, *"I Accept This Challenge!"*.

Congratulations, you are now enlisted as a soldier of the Global Food Revolution!

Key Points:

- *The disastrous twins called world hunger and poverty are approaching with freight train speed. War is inevitable for nations who run out of food or fresh water. A Global Food Revolution is required NOW.*

- *Impassioned individuals to the importance of food security can impact communities, cities, nations – to become "world changers". Will that be You? You are being called into the revolutionary army of the Global Food Revolution!*

―――――――

"If you want to eliminate hunger, everybody has to be involved." Bono

―――――――

Chapter 1

Food Shortages Are Increasing

"The lives of millions of people depend on our collective ability to act. In our world of plenty, there is no excuse for inaction or indifference."

Antonio Guterrez, UN Secretary General

The reports keep coming in and they are pointing towards a future of massive global food insecurity. Populations are growing at an unprecedented rate, set to reach 9.8 billion people by 2050 and 11.2 billion by 2100. Unfortunately, farmland production is not expanding to the degree needed to meet the current and coming world food demands. Couple these statistics with social, geo-political and even weather disruptions in various parts of the world, and we have many crisis scenarios forming right now in front of us, our children, and our grandchildren!

Certain areas of the world are going to suffer more than others. Some areas will become food growing baskets for the rest of the world. Some areas will become barren, needy and hungry to the point of riots, wars and starvation of the populations. Mass migration could be the only viable solution for some. Those too poor to migrate will meet their own demise.

Can you believe that wars in the future will be fought over food, natural resources, and available water? When desperation levels rise, people are forced to fight for survival, for their families, and communities. Various nations are already fighting for water rights over multi-national flowing rivers. Try building a river dam in your nation and see what the next nation downstream has planned for you. These skirmishes are already in the works. Egypt has condemned Ethiopia's Nile mega dam project, threatening war if the project continues. Look around. Nations are preparing for water shortages and are looking for natural resources that could be acquired (legally and illegally). Everywhere I go, I hear the professionals saying that the two buzz words of the 21st century are FOOD and WATER. I think it's important that you and I take action on these two words before any crisis arises, especially near or around us.

Let's take a look at powerful statements from key groups and individuals.

The Food Security Information Network released their GLOBAL REPORT 2017 ON FOOD CRISIS, and the conclusion was, *"Currently, the world is faced with an unprecedented call for action"... The numbers of people facing food insecurity are on the rise, caused primarily by conflict, record high food prices and abnormal weather patterns."*

José Graziano da Silva, FAO Director-General said, *"We can prevent people dying from famine but if we do not scale up our efforts to save, protect and invest in rural livelihoods, tens of millions will remain severely food insecure."*

Ms. Federica Mogherini, High Representative of the Union for Foreign Affairs and Security Policy and Vice President of the European Commission said, *"Leaving no one behind is a moral and political duty,* and requires political will. Working in partnership is the best guarantee for addressing this common challenge in a globalized world."

Ertharin Cousin, Executive Director of the United Nations World Food Programme said, "The numbers tell a deeply worrying story. It is a race against time - we need to act now to save the lives and livelihoods of the millions at the brink of starvation today. "

Lester Brown, President of the Earth Policy Research Centre in Washington, said, "Armed aggression is no longer the principal threat to our future. The overriding threats to this century are climate change, population growth, spreading water shortages and rising food prices."

In 2015 the United Nations Food Report said, "The world needs to produce at least 50% more food to feed 9 billion people by 2050. But climate change could cut crop yields by more than 25%. The land, biodiversity, oceans, forests, and other forms of natural capital are being depleted at unprecedented rates. Unless we change how we grow our food and manage our natural capital, food security—especially for the world's poorest—will be at risk.

A 2017 article in "Strategy + Business" titled "Innovation from Farm to Table" By Barry Jaruzelski, Volker Staack, Tom Jonson, says, "The urgent need for such R&D investment cannot be overstated. The United Nations estimates that by 2050, the world's population will reach 9.7 Billion. Ensuring adequate supplies of food will require a 70 percent increase in agricultural production over the next 30 years. These numbers present the global agricultural sector with a daunting task, especially when they are combined with the effects of climate change and resource scarcity. Already today, in parts of Africa and the Middle East, millions of people are on the brink of famine. In the past, production growth largely came from increasing the amount of land and labor in use. But it is now clear that the amount of arable land available will not keep pace with demand. We need to be able to produce more with the land we have, while being mindful of resource scarcity and the potential for environmental degradation."

Grow Intelligence founder and chief executive Sra Menker says the world could be facing a food shortage in just 10 years, and that 2023 is the crossover point where we will no longer be able to produce enough food to feed a growing global population.

Gerald C. Nelson is Professor Emeritus at the University of Illinois at Urbana-Champaign and former senior research fellow at the international food policy research institute. His team studies conclude: "Micronutrient shortages such as Vitamin A deficiency are already causing blindness in 250,000 and 500,000 children a year and killing half of them within 12 months of them losing their sight. Dietary shortages of iron, zinc, iodine and folate all have devastating health effects.

Our success with (growing and providing) carbohydrates has had a serious downside: a worldwide plague of obesity, diabetes and other diet-related diseases. The World Health Organization reports that in 2014, there were 462 million underweight adults worldwide but more than 600 million who were obese — nearly two-thirds of them in *developing* countries. And childhood obesity is rising much faster in poorer countries than in richer ones.

These statistics point to the need for more emphasis on nutrients other than carbohydrates in our diets. Our findings thus point to the need for a course correction. We must shift our emphasis from **food security** to **nutrition security**."

Every organization and professional who studies food security, population growth, global weather disruptions and future sustainability risk will tell you that we are quickly approaching a cataclysmic nightmare scenario of epic proportions. Our world is needlessly running out of food, while our populations are growing and expanding. Different organizations present different dates for total collapse of global food security. Some say as early as 2025 we will see significant problems. Others point towards 2030 or even 2050. But the fact remains the same that most of us will see in our lifetimes, a worldwide shortage of food and global conflict because of nations' positioning for food and clean water for their populations. However, this can be alleviated if we will join the Global Food Revolution. If you and I will put our hands to the proverbial plow, we can help alleviate this coming catastrophic global food crisis. Let's roll up our sleeves and get to work, for the sake of love, humanity, and our next generation of children.

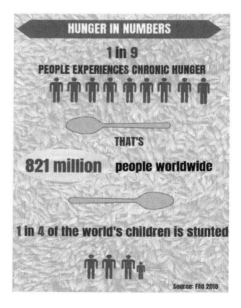

Look at this UN chart. With these facts in front of us from their 2018 report, we can see how easily the 'one out of nine' present statistics can turn to two or three out of nine, simply with population explosion and lack of farm land expansion. And looking back in history, the U.N. numbers are growing each year instead of shrinking.

I have been educating with four facts and a wildcard that verify this chart.

Fact 1: population explosion, 9.7 billion by 2050.

Fact 2: Instead of growing 50% more food by 2030, we are growing less on declining, useable farmlands.

Fact 3: Agricultural technology has stalled and is not keeping up with global demand to produce more food.

Fact 4: New super bugs and disease are wiping out entire regional crops and herds.

Wild Card: Long term weather pattern shifts and climate changes are wreaking havoc on farmlands and growing cycles and seasons.

These four facts and the Wild card stand in front of us clearly indicating that we need a full Global Food Revolution.

- *Population growth is vastly exceeding the world's food sustainability, which is further decimated by social, geopolitical variables, technology hindrances, superbugs and unprecedented changing global weather patterns.*

- *Famine is confronting various nations and people groups even as you read this book. Together, we can work to alleviate local and international disasters through the Global Food Revolution.*

Hunger is actually the worst weapon of mass destruction. It claims millions of victims each year." Luiz Inacio Lula da Silva, President of Brazil

---

Chapter 2

United Nations "Zero Hunger" Mandate

If you will search the internet for the "United Nations Global Food Crisis Report" or "Zero Hunger Challenge", you will find some of the target objectives of the U.N. Their data is conclusive and as I read their information and goals, I see that the U.N. is ready for a Global Food Revolution. They will be calling on all nations to join this revolution. Get on board now, or get on board later. Soon everyone will be on board. Let's lead the way.

The United Nations "Zero Hunger Challenge" launched in 2012 gives a tall order to citizens of the globe. Their targeted goals within a generation are:

- Zero stunted children under the age of two
- 100% access to adequate food all year round
- All food systems are sustainable
- 100% increase in smallholder productivity and income
- Zero loss or waste of food

What noble goals and targeted directives these are. And they are fully achievable within our generation. But massive revolution and total change of the entire current system and way of thinking is required. In a way, everything you and I think today of food from farm to table "must" and "will" change. And when I say change, I mean "total Global Food Revolution".

Each of these 5 goals will require mass innovation, entrepreneurialism, and education of the masses. If the U.N. is to achieve these hard targets within this generation, we will certainly be re-thinking how we grow, transport, package, buy, consume and preserve food on a global scale.

Let's break down each of these targets.

#1. Zero stunted children under the age of two

In order to facilitate a nutritional package to every child around the world from ages 0 – 2, we must decide what adequate infant nutrition means, then develop systematic ways to grow, process, package and deliver this nutrition to every planetary household. I'm sure this may include breast feeding to a certain age, then a required nutrient rich food that will help every baby grow correctly in their first 2 years. Who will pay for this? Unless the income level of the extreme poor increases dramatically, someone else is going to pay for this mandate. I won't speculate on who will pay this bill. But there will certainly be funds and resources available to the right people who develop this in their areas, nations or internationally.

I don't personally believe that we can just plan to teach people to grow their nutrition and hit the U.N. "Zero Stunted Children" target. People are uneducated, unprepared and some are lazy. Many will not make it a priority to provide nutrition, even if it was handed to them. The revolutionary system must include education, incentive and access to nutrition. This is the truly sustainable method to train every parent in the world. God help us!

That system must reach every location in the world, from the peak villages of the Himalayan Mountains at 16,000 feet to the farthest tribal hut in the

Amazon of Latin America. It will be cheap, portable, easily produced, shelf stable, palatable and never lacking in supply (being very food secure and sustainable).

This mandate #1 is shouting out for entrepreneurial companies to arise and tackle global demand. If someone can complete part or all of this mandate, it is a multibillion dollar company just waiting to be formed with government, U.N., educational, institutional and nonprofit organization help. Just imagine what must be coming in the future to meet mandate #1.

#2. 100% access to adequate food all year round

Global access to adequate food 12 months per year will require nutritional production, packaging, distribution and delivery systems and a defining of what "adequate food" really means for various regions, zones and cultures. Providing for global zones which can only produce food three to six months per year will be a technological challenge. A combination of new technologies, investment capital, mass innovation and out of the box thinking will be required.

It's reported that the residents of the Himalayan mountains at 15,000 – 16,000 feet altitude have a 90-day annual growing season. Many global regions have a 180 day per year growing season. There are local and regional challenges, weather anomalies and even cultural hindrances that we must overcome. It will require grass roots heart, passion, education and capacity to innovate.

We will need to crack wide open our FACT #3 *(Chapter 1: 4 facts and a wild card)* with advanced technology to meet this U.N. hard target.

#3. All food systems are sustainable

Let's get a good handle on what "sustainability" really means so we can look at this U.N. hard target correctly.

Wikipedia says: Sustainability is the process of maintaining change in a balanced fashion, in which the exploitation of resources, the direction of investments, the orientation of technological development and institutional change are all in harmony and enhance both current and future potential to meet human needs and aspirations.

Dictionary.com defines sustainable as:
*"Capable of being supported or upheld, as by having its weight borne from below.
*Pertaining to a system that maintains its own viability by using techniques that allow for continual reuse: *sustainable agriculture.*
Aquaculture is a sustainable alternative to overfishing.
*Able to be maintained or kept going, as an action or process: *a sustainable negotiation between the two countries.*
*Able to be confirmed or upheld: *a sustainable decision.*

*Able to be supported as with the basic necessities or sufficient funds: *a sustainable life."*

Sustainability is basically a system that produces as much or more energy than it takes to create and maintain it.

The Sun Model:

I have used my own idea of sustainability when looking at any venture, business opportunity, or ideology. I see the greatest business model of all time hanging in the day time sky. It's called the sun. If you study the sun as a business model, you will find a masterful business plan that is fully sustainable. And it seems to me to be the model of sustainability for the entire world. It's not easy to develop businesses, farms, and projects after the order of the sun. But I am convinced that it's possible if you dig deep enough and get far enough out of the box of standard, general thinking. For me, if the system cannot meet the model of the sustainable sun, I abandon the project and move onward. Why live in failed models when we can develop sustainable models? It doesn't make sense to me.

Photo by William Picard, https://freeimages.com

To make the study short and to the point, the sun was created and hung in the sky on Day 4 of creation according to the Holy Bible. It was lit on fire one time. And from that day forward, it has recreated itself and continued in a sustainable fashion from its beginning until now.

The sun's gases heat up at the center, push towards the surface and release their heat energy. And as they cool they rotate to the center again to start the cycle over. The energy released is a gift to all living things as the heat and light of the sun's energy cause massive life to prosper and multiply on earth and beyond.

The gift of energy is something to be received and managed. There's nothing we can do to stop it. And fortunately for all of us, mankind can't go to the sun and try to tweak its business model to make it better. The sun continues to give and give, and to recreate itself over and over, century after millennium.

This is the perfect model of sustainability. If we would follow this model in our business and management capacities on earth, we would become sustainable in many new ways. The U.N. mandate #3 requires that we think outside of our old failed, unsustainable, antiquated, self-constructed boxes, and to transform our systems to fully sustainable systems. This is full Global Food Revolution.

Now, breaking down the U.N. objective to make all food systems sustainable, we realize that we must perfect the management skills of food production.

Fact #3 Technology *(Chapter 1: 4 Facts & a Wild Card)* must be reinvented and kick started again with a fresh understanding, "out of the box" thinking, and willingness to press the envelope of sustainability at all costs. When I say at all costs, I mean the cost of getting out of the box in our thinking and willingness to abandon the old and embrace the new pathways. Because when we find and embrace the sustainable path, it will sustain itself with no further input or cost.

There are systems on our planet that haven't yet been created or developed. They are waiting for creative people and companies to formulate "sun model" food growing and delivery systems that create small input and give out huge output using the power of seed, multiplication, science, and engineering in less time than in previous antiquated systems. Peripheral concepts and entire industries must be created and developed to make our world totally sustainable.

This means, "out with the old and in with the new" in some instances. The old will be challenged with new concepts and capacities which the old cannot facilitate.

This is a new day for creative people and companies looking to invest into the next generation. The potential is waiting. The United Nations is calling for you to step up to the plate and innovate, develop and design a sustainable future for mankind. Not only will you create the platform for the masses to live and succeed, but you will create company based systems that will totally replace some of the old, outdated multi-billion dollar companies that are currently entrenched in our world.

#4. 100% increase in smallholder productivity and income

Once again the United Nations is calling for the development and creation of technologies that will multiply the productivity and income of the small farmer, producer and distributor of nutrition around the world. When these technologies emerge on the scene and when they include the small holder rather than only giant corporations, the global food crisis will shift into neutral very quickly. When farmers make 100% more than they are today, new farmers will emerge globally to join the Global Food Revolution as a sustainable way that they can feed their families, pay bills, and create wealth. Farmlands will be activated "en masse" and the agricultural sector will boom.

In order for small holders to experience a 100% increase in productivity and income, I can only foresee a couple of ways from my present vantage point. First, new technologies and ease of multiplication has to become accessible to the small holder. And second, the prices of food must increase, or the costs of technology, fertilizers, salaries, supplies and equipment must drop significantly. We may need a combination of the two. This would mean a full revolution of current agricultural systems, and in some ways would mean a collapse or complete reshaping of those old systems that are currently in place.

I was having a conversation one day with a friend in Panama how the farmers in Panama were suffering horribly. Frequently what happens is that the farmer gets ready to bring their onions or other produce to market, but just before they harvest, multiple container loads of onions hit the dock from other nations. This sinks the national price of onions from $80 per hundred pounds to $15 per hundred pounds. At that point, the farmer can't even afford to pay the workers to harvest the onions and they remain in the field at a total loss to the farmer. This is heart breaking to see over and over again.

While I was complaining about this, my friend spoke up and said, "It sounds like Panama needs a full global food revolution. Why can other nations grow onions for $15 per hundred pounds when our farmers need $80 per hundred pounds to grow them?"

When I heard this, something inside of me stood up and shouted, "Pay attention!".

While there are multiple facets to this problem and story, we have to take a second look at this scenario. If someone else is growing cheap onions that can be exported to other nations at $15 per hundred pounds, maybe we need to be educated on what we can grow in Panama at a good, profitable price that we can export to the nations at a price that makes everyone a "winner". Is it possible that we need a Global Food Revolution with global farming and allocation of produce, assets and vision? Maybe we need to learn how to grow $15 per hundred pound onions? Someone is doing it and possibly making a profit. But make sure that the onions are the same quality rather than inferior, stripped down, non-nutritional versions of the real thing. Are they real onions at $15 per hundred pounds, or simply onion cadavers from the old world that have no nutrition and are laced with toxic waste? Or are they liquidation onions that need to find a quick home at a cheap price, though it will destroy the local farmers wherever they land?

Governments do need to protect their farmers through regulation and other creative systems. But it's very probable that the Global Food Revolution will require rethinking at the farm level like we have never imagined before. This is what revolution is all about. A total rethinking and retooling of the way we do business.

Revolution: noun. A sudden, complete or marked change in something.

With this understanding, we can move forward to help make farmers more productive and more wealthy. Remember that we need to be supporting the small holder of agriculture regardless the price of the food. Small holder agriculture is a calling, not a cash cow. Their passion, hard work and willingness to take massive risk results in you and me being able to eat great quality foods, grown locally.

Are you well fed? When's the last time you thanked your farmer? Thank them, and help those small farmers to have 100% more productivity and income. It's mandated in our future. It's going to happen. If you have joined the Global Food Revolution, you need to start a "Thank a Farmer" project of some kind now.

#5. Zero loss or waste of food

The first four hard targets of the U.N. are technology based and require massive advancement and development. But this fifth target is actually looking backwards to a great degree. Yes, all new sustainable developments must have built into them zero loss.

With this U.N. mandate #5, we can actually attack a current problem that we have globally, and bring great benefit. Namely, we are losing 40% of food produced globally to accident, inclement weather, rot or general mismanagement of that food. This happens every day at farm, distribution, store and home levels.

As I travel the globe, some of the farm enemies that I see which cause farmers to lose 10%-15% of their crops include blight, weather, rodents, negative markets, or harvest problems among other farm enemies. The distributor, packaging company and grocery store can lose as much as 10%-15% through low sales, rot, or accident of the food handling process. And the end user/customer loses 10% in many cases as the food went to waste before it could be eaten.

While we are pressing hard to grow 50% more food in the coming years to meet global demand, we can look back and attempt to save the food that we're already growing. If there was a way to save all of the 40% crop loss, then our need to grow more food is greatly diminished going forward. And the U.N. is mandating that we look at all food waste and develop a plan to stop it. All of it! This will require a total rethinking of our current systems in place and the way we grow, package, distribute, buy and consume food.

This U.N. mandate gives great opportunity to innovators, designers and developers to create new systems of zero waste on the farm, in transport, at the factory, in the grocery store and at home. The capacity to save and preserve food is a hard target mandate. What do we do with the bell pepper that falls off of the vine at the farm, or the pepper that begins to shrivel before it can be used, whether at the store or in the home?

I personally see many great opportunities here with dehydration and freeze drying of foods. Farm dehydrators and commercial systems as well as small at home units the size of a microwave oven will help take us to zero waste.

Nonprofit organizations can also develop ways to capture food loss by developing gleaning systems that will mobilize volunteer help to cut/slice/dice, dehydrate and distribute foods that are at the edge of being too ripe or old. Fast delivery systems to the poor will become powerful nonprofit systems that society will embrace and support.

Other technologies will potentially arise in the future to add value and food preservation time. These technologies and innovations are dependent on individuals, companies, and revolutionary groups to take the challenge and rise to the occasion.

As members of the Global Food Revolution, we can do our part to thrust the U.N. Zero Hunger challenge in our own lives, families, neighborhoods, cities and nations. Education, activism, passion and willingness to help others is critical. Help educate your relational base on why they need to also join the Global Food Revolution.

Here are some areas that you can actively take part in to join the U.N. Zero Hunger challenge as a member of the Global Food Revolution?

#1. Zero stunted children under the age of two

Sponsor a nutritional program for a poor and needy child in the first or third world. Volunteer with a nonprofit organization who works with children and nutrition. Sponsor an infant in your city who is not getting proper care. Reach out and offer your world new ideas and innovation. Get proactive and creative.

#2. 100% access to adequate food all year round

Join groups, nonprofits or global teams that are making a difference in impoverished parts of the world, near or abroad. Help communities reach new goals of having access to nutrition twelve months out of the year. Be even more courageous - taking an agricultural tour vacation and roll up your sleeves to help in the third world. Get proactive and creative.

#3. All food systems are sustainable

Re-examine and thereby take a second look at your own food system. Rethink whether or not your food sources are sustainable. If not, develop a program that will help you grow your own super foods or store an emergency supply of food. Reconsider how you purchase your foods to end all waste. Have a plan for everything before it goes to waste. Learn ways to preserve and fight to stop all waste as a new way of revolutionary life.

#4. 100% increase in smallholder productivity and income

Support your local farmers. Look for local farmer's markets and make it a point to go spend money there. Pay more money for good quality foods grown locally. From time to time, tip your local farmer and adopt a farmer as your own. Find and follow your local farmers. Help them to increase and expand. Offer to help them invest further into farming and new technologies. Give or rent them some of your unused land. Become creative and active. Care for them like never before. Remember, farming is a calling, not a cash cow. There is a reason that the U.N. is mandating that small holder farmers make 100% more than they are making today.

#5. Zero loss or waste of food

Rethink how you are buying your food and how much is actually going to waste. If you could reduce your waste by 10%, you could afford to pay 10% more to your local farmer group without ever spending more money. Consider buying a dehydrator or freeze drying unit. Dehydrators are cheap. When you see a shriveling tomato or pepper, it's helping you start the dehydration process. Capture the nutrition and suspend the value of that food for up to a year by dehydrating. Add your extras into recipes and soups. Brainstorm, alone or with the help of others to develop and activate a plan of action for you personally and/or your family to utilize. Look at food as calories and nutrition, and protect that investment with proper care. It's a new way of thinking and a new life style that must be established in order to fulfill mandate #5. Do it, and teach it to others quickly. It's our responsibility to change the world and make it sustainable for everyone through lifestyle changes.

I implore you to take hold of these targets and create a pathway to personal, family, community and global success. There is room in the Global Food Revolution for millions of ideas, inventions and innovations to help reach the Zero Hunger Challenge in this generation, which includes the young upcoming generation of young people around us.

Let's get busy.

Key Points:

- *The 2012 UN Global Food Crisis Report – Zero Hunger Challenge is focusing on children, adequate food, sustainable systems, smallholder productivity increase, and zero food loss or waste.*

- *Using the sun model, new innovative, sustainable technologies must be created to propel the Global Food Revolution.*

———————

"There are genuinely sufficient resources in the world to ensure that no one, nowhere, at no time, should go hungry." Ed Asner

———————

Chapter 3

Weather Disruptions Are Increasing

Some call it "Global Warming". Some call it "Global Cooling" and others call it "Climate Change". I call it the "Wild Card". Some scientists are screaming that a "Grand Solar Minimum" and a cyclical mini ice age are here. Others believe it's a "manmade" crisis. One believes it's heating and the other believes its cooling. Of course they all have their scientists on hand to prove both sides of the coin. One thing that everyone seems to agree on is that our global weather patterns are shifting and causing chaos around the world. In past global history these seasons of weather pattern shifts were responsible for the fall of dynasties, mass migration, starvation and population reduction. This was primarily because of the disruption of food supplies. These weather pattern shifts mean that chaos and havoc have once again surfaced for food growers around the world. It looks like these disruptions are here to stay for the long term (at least for our life span).

Today's news reports are a continuing saga of weather disruptions to come. Record snowfall is hitting around the world. Recently shepherds in Europe were seen on video digging their sheep out of a huge two-meter blanket of snow that came unexpectedly in October, 2018. Blistering worldwide records pertaining to snow and cold were set during 2018/2019 winter months as extreme temperatures hit hard and early in the season. In 2018, Canada's early flash freeze left their seed potato crop frozen in the ground. Germany reported the worst potato crops in history in 2018. as well. In Sicily, Italy in 2019, a one-night super storm destroyed their entire crop productions, marked as a "death sentence" for farmers.

36

In October, 2018, growers in the UK were warning of shortages of onions, potatoes and other vegetables after extreme weather destroyed crops across the nation. Also in 2018, temperatures hit -18F in Northern India, destroying 70% - 80% of apple orchards. In Southern India, Munnar lost 800 hectares of tea production for a second year in a row as new weather patterns were established over that region.

Wild fires, droughts, and even volcanic eruptions with plumes of ash are cooling the atmosphere. Jet stream changes are stopping the flow of oceanic waters causing disruptions in the north. On and on we can go with super storms, cat 5 hurricanes and a Mexico hurricane that strengthened while traveling over land through a desert! Since when does that happen?

2019 brought a polar vortex through Northern USA that killed 1 million cattle burying many in 8 feet of snow to the demise of many generational farms. The ensuing melting snow brought floods that wiped out 1 million + acres of farmland, totally obliterating the stored corn reserves, and sent many farmers into crisis mode while entire farm towns went under water. Farmlands since then have been too wet to plant, resulting in a devastating blow to the nations' corn supplies.

A new super cyclone just hit Mozambique, killing thousands, entirely destroying hundreds of villages, and trapping people in trees and on rooftops for up to 10 days without food or water. Helicopters and rescue boats ran night and day to save as many as possible. After the flood waters receded, survivors went back to their villages to try to relocate their farmlands and get some seed in the ground before the arrival of winter. The risk of mass starvation would be a reality if they could not harvest quickly.

However, just months after the first cyclone, another mass cyclone event destroyed crops and fields again.

Australia just pulled in all wheat exports because of a potential 30-year drought that could change their nation. As the jet stream has shifted south, it has pushed cyclone activity away from Australia used to enjoy the rains which were responsible for bountiful wheat crops. Those rains are now gone. Australia was the #2 exporter of wheat to Africa. Now what does Africa do? Bread is the major staple of the African diet. How will this be made up and who will provide it? Could wheat go to the highest bidder in the future, pricing the poor out of their historically available staple foods?

The Bahamas just suffered a massive crippling Cat 5 hurricane (Dorian) with sustained 185 mph winds and a 23-foot storm surge. This monster hurricane STOPPED over Bahamas for 36 hours before continuing onward. We had an active plan to develop a super food project on the Abaco Islands in Bahamas just weeks before the hurricane hit. But since the hurricane, Abaco was decimated and scores of its farmers were swept away to meet their demise. We now must not only redevelop their farmlands, but we need to find new farmers, supporting survivors of this great tragedy!

Too many of these catastrophes could create a perfect storm that could thrust our world into global famine with food prices sky rocketing out of reach for the poor and even the middle class.

We must be ready to face the strong possibility that the jet stream could be radically changing course for a long time. Oceans could heat or cool, ice caps shrink or gain, rainfall could stall over certain areas or long term droughts could strike.

There is strong science that shows solar cycles and corresponding earth cycles that mirror the beginning of a mini ice age. The science behind this current mini ice age is calling for up to 300 years of global cooling! If this were to happen in our lifetimes, the potential for starvation, suffering and death is very high during extreme winter months. Billions could lose their lives because they can't get out of the way of a changing climate. New (much lower) temperatures during winter could make parts of the world uninhabitable and crop failures would be catastrophic. This would result in the collapse of society, industries, cities and nations. "Total global upheaval" would be too kind to describe this kind of collapse.

Today's solar cycles seem to be mirroring the Maunder Minimum in the 17th century. During that time, rivers and canals froze in Northern Europe for months during the winter with ice being over one foot in thickness. The Baltic Sea froze over and crop failure and famines were wide spread during this time. A decline in solar activity is most easily measured in the decline of sun spots observed as the sun cycles into dormancy. During the Maunder Minimum, this solar decline brought deep freezing winter temperatures for decades.

Wikipedia says: During a 28-year period (1672–1699) within the Maunder Minimum, observations revealed fewer than 50 sunspots. This contrasts with the typical 40000 – 50000 sunspots seen in modern times (over similar 25 year sampling).[8] Like the Dalton Minimum and the Sporer Minimum, the Maunder Minimum coincided with a period of lower-than-average European temperatures.

Further study of the Maunder Minimum reveals non conclusive evidence that the lack of sun spots was directly linked to colder temperatures. But studies at Technical University of Denmark and the Hebrew University of Jerusalem have linked solar activity to Earth's cloud cover which can affect global temperatures. The current best hypothesis for the cause of the Little Ice Age is that it was the result of volcanic action which can increase cloud cover on the planet. Yes, solar activity can potentially cause volcanoes to activate and earthquakes to increase.

Grand Solar Minimum science says that we entered a cyclical mini ice age in 2016. Since then we have seen many strange occurrences in the weather, many volcanoes activating and earthquake data that's off the charts. Experts anticipate that record breaking cold and snowfall is coming earlier and stronger. Stalled weather patterns and droughts are setting within new locations. Super storms, cyclones, and hurricanes are bringing great devastation with stronger winds. Certainly the climate is changing. But what does this mean for us?

If we were to repeat the last Grand Solar Minimums, we can only hope that new technologies, creative ideas, and hard working entrepreneurs would be able to save us from total catastrophic collapse. If streams, lakes, rivers and oceans freeze over, what would the inhabitants of those areas do? Will the electrical grids stay up to keep vital infrastructure in place? Will food and water supplies continue through the cold seasons? Can trucking, air and shipping transportation continue? If snow falls heavy during the coming winters, will this result in massive flooding as in the USA during 2018? Will rainfall continue during the spring and summer? Will populations, industries and agriculture be able to buckle down and adapt to the global changes? Indeed, everything we have considered normal may be tested over and over again. Every current boundary line may be tested and moved. And when those old norms break, the global community must be in position to help those who are in critical and desperate need. This includes developing transportation of foods and supplies into frozen zones and helping people insulate and harden their living quarters. Food, water, supplies and transportation will be crucial if this new paradigm is to succeed. Governments must be ready to change regulations to protect life. People may need to burn wood in some areas to keep warm. Others may need to collect rain water to survive. Many industries including animal and plant farming may have to move to warmer zones to survive multiple decades (or centuries) of global cooling. This would reduce or eliminate jobs in the cold zones. The cold could quite literally cause pandemics, panic, and mass migration to warmer climates. Not all will have the sustenance to provide for their move.

Again, I am a novice when looking at climate disruptions. There are scientists that show the earth is warming. Many believe that the polar ice caps could melt which would raise ocean levels and change our entire international seaboards with permanent flooding of the coastal areas. I wish I knew whether we are going into global cooling or warming. But I am positive that we are going into "Climate Craziness", and that is the wildcard that can change life on earth.

Today's Global Food Revolution must prepare for climate change, whether warming, cooling or a combination of both. New technologies require that we learn to grow food indoors, underground, and using solar, wind or alternative power if possible. We must pursue LED or other compatible lighting. We must search for new advancements that can grow mass protein and carbohydrates in new, more sustainable and controllable environments. We will need to adapt our crop growing to the new climates of our areas. Some crops don't grow well in heat or cold. Most don't grow well in drought stricken areas. High winds and new storms can wreak havoc on agriculture as a whole. As outside weather becomes hostile and radical, indoor growing may be required in certain areas to sustain life.

In the third world, many "at risk" people could simply starve or freeze to death, given the scenarios above. Many communities are not prepared for a 20F – 50F degree drop in winter temperatures or a 20F – 50F raise in temperatures during summer. Accordingly, they would not survive a prolonged drought or stalled weather patterns that last for forty to three hundred years. These "at risk" people groups must be trained and educated now to learn new forms of agriculture, new ways to grow food, and new ways to protect their families, farms and future. I am most worried about many of these people groups when considering climate change. Billions are at risk without the capacity to make changes and embrace new technologies needed to save their lives. Indeed, humanity will need to give sacrificially and provide education and help towards these most vulnerable, including widows and orphans who are normally the first to suffer and die when troubles like these come.

Nobility always triumphs over necessity. If we act now out of nobility, we can help save the world from a lot of pain, suffering and death. But if we wait until we MUST change out of necessity, then countless lives could be lost and our necessity will be their calamity. - Dr. Daniel Daves

---

Climate change will require a change of lifestyle for everyone on the planet. If we don't plan to change, we will pay dearly as food prices rise in the future. We will live and eat differently. We will embrace new technologies and will adapt to the new weather of the future. If not, we first go broke, then we die. But if we do adapt, we can actually advance humanity and become better global managers of our planet. We can bring forward new technologies that could birth a global food renaissance. This could transform our world and bring sustainable food production to a new level for humanity! The choice is ours.

We must consider what we can do to prepare for climate change. The sooner we act, the better off you and your family will be and the less expensive the changes will cost us all going into the future.

You, your family, and community will need new education, new technologies, and the power to know how to grow your own food. Depending on where you live and how the climate changes in your zone, you may need to move. Your job or business could be in jeopardy. Your future may need to revolve around adaptability. Certainly our planet is changing its seasons and these changes will affect the entire world. Don't delay. Each news report of a new super storm, cyclone, hurricane, drought, flooding or record snow is talking to you.

Many corporations and companies are moving assets and making plans for a very different food growing and climate future in food production. If you knew the corporate movements that the main stream media is not currently reporting, you would be shocked!

Del Monte is currently divesting itself this year out of their canning facilities in North America. In other words, they are taking an "asset light" position during this climate craziness season as higher risks abound. Del Monte just closed three canning factories in northern USA, including a corn packing plant in northern Illinois, a plant in Sleepy Eye, MN and one in Cambria, WI. (Note these are all in northern USA). After this canning season, the plants will be closed and employees sent home. *(Update: Sleepy Eye plant has been bought in an attempt to keep it open.)* Interestingly, Del Monte is moving their packing facilities from USA to Kenya, Africa. China is also moving facilities to Kenya. Big money is moving to areas where food can be grown in the future. Why?

In 2018 Cargill had to close grain plants in St. Louis, MO and in South Dakota due to extreme cold temperatures. Cargill is divesting within North America, and specifically selling thirteen of their grain and crop assets in Ontario. Why?

Ardent Mills are closing four flour mills which are going off line in the USA. They are also closing a barely to malt processing plant in Jamestown, North Dakota. On the other hand, the company is now investing in factories in Ecuador, South America that can produce bacteria to feed fish and livestock. Why?

In Weirton, West Virginia, the Arcelor-Mittal steel mill (United Steel Workers) just laid off 100 employees in August 2019 because there was no more need for tin cans due to poor crop harvests and a lack of food to can in the north.

If large corporations are taking profits, selling off production facilities in the North, and moving investments to warmer crop growing climates, what types of actions should you be thinking about?

During climate craziness, earthquakes and active volcanoes have a strong potential of increasing their global activity. And if enough volcanoes go active, the earth cools just from increased volcanic clouds in the atmosphere.

Coupling our mass population increase with reduction of usable farm lands, and then throwing the wild card of climate change, means we must be prepared for a very different future than we have known.

Key Points:

- *Weather disruptions, including record freezing and heat, cyclonic activity, hurricanes and drought are causing unrestrained chaos has resulted in mass migration, starvation, population reduction with devastating loss of crops and food.*

- *Food corporations and companies have moved assets with plans to grow differently, in warmer climates to avoid financial ruin, where possible. Being adaptable with openness to change may be necessary to participate in the Global Food Revolution.*

"A hungry man is not a free man." Adlai E. Stevenson

Chapter 4

Food Revolution for the Small Farmer

"The local farmer has been bailing us out and has subsidized the low price of our foods for decades. Why? So we can eat cheap, eat all we want, and spend our money elsewhere on ourselves. Our food bail outs are about over, and our cheap food is about to disappear! – Dr. Daniel Daves"

I have seen it for decades and it seems to be increasing. Governments and corporations frequently unite to create agricultural business deals that benefit a few, and enslave many more. This is an international problem. Many times the small local farmer takes repeated massive hits for profitable corporate deals that take place at a higher level. And sometimes local farmers have no choice but to fold and give up farming because they just can't compete with their governments and big corporate farming. Or they embrace the chains of their slavery in hope of change and freedom sometime in the future. And what's more, the small farmer is trying to compete against a totally unsustainable large scale business model which strips the land of valuable mineral content, strips food of proper nutrition, and destroys the sustainability of the small farmer at the same time. I will be brutally clear and precise in a moment. But first, a short reminder of some of the current priorities of the United Nations World Food Programme, World Bank, Food and Agricultural Organization, and International Fund for Agricultural Development.

These entities are stating their absolute resolve to bring sustainable global change to food production. They are calling for nothing less than a Global Food Revolution. Here are just a few of their stated intentions:

- Doubling the agricultural productivity and incomes of small-scale food producers;
- Ensuring sustainable food production systems;
- Increasing investment in agriculture;
- Correcting and preventing trade restrictions and distortions in world agricultural markets;
- Adopting measures to ensure the proper functioning of food commodity markets.

In today's world of large corporate agriculture and misdirected government oversight, high level decisions work hand in hand to make the small food producer unsustainable, unprofitable and incapable of producing good, nutritious foods at a reasonable price. The catastrophic results of misuse of government power (local, state, federal and international) have destroyed entire swaths of small farmers and food producers. Corporate greed at high levels have cut many corners to the detriment of sound food nutrition, safety, and sustainability. They are famous for driving artificial food prices so low that very few small providers can survive in their wake. This is a true nightmare happening under our watch around the globe. It's unsustainable, it's immoral, and it must be confronted in your locality. If not confronted, entire people groups will pay dearly, potentially with their lives cut short when the unsustainable factors come into play and their food systems break in half. There will not be enough time to make the corrections necessary to regain production needed to provide sufficient nutrition for their populations.

As a small farmer myself, I want to stand up for small farmers for a moment. When we developed our prototype farm in Panama, we began learning about the local and national economy in relation to food production. We found out that it was nearly impossible to make enough money to pay the bills, let alone ever make a profit. Though Panama tax laws allowed a farm to make up to $250,000 per year tax free, we found that most, if not all farmers were not making $1 profit after a year's worth of hard work, paying salaries, plant foods and soil amendments, fuel, and capital costs such as greenhouses, wells, vehicles, tractors and other equipment. After a few years of production, we found that it was our new dream to try to break even rather than make a profit. And in breaking even, that didn't mean that the owner received anything for his 55 hours per week involvement, capital investment and management of the farm. When the dream of future success is reduced to one's attempts to break even, something is desperately wrong with that business model. It's absolutely unsustainable. This is not an investment in which any sane person would want to invest. It's actually a black hole of poverty which eventually results in the small farmer breaking, giving up, living in mass poverty, and giving in to illicit or illegal activities to subsidize the farm. It will also result in a lowering of ethics in order to survive, including "screwing thy neighbor" in whatever way necessary in order to make enough to pay the bills and put food on the table. This spirit of poverty breeds lawlessness, mistrust, anti-community and hopelessness within an agricultural community.

Not only does all of this exist in our local world, but we have found it to exist internationally in so many nations that we have visited. It is all part of an antiquated, corrupted, unsustainable business model that will eventually break if we don't bring systemic change now.

In 2019, Central American Data released a horrific news report titled, "Agricultural Production in Danger of Extinction". Panama is the nation that our prototype farm is located in! Yet the Panama farmer is in danger of extinction? How do you survive as a farmer in a climate that is threatening your very existence? Only through a Global Food Revolution!

The small farmer is in deep trouble around the world! Many farmers pay $2 to sell $1 worth of vegetables. Many of them are forced to use highly toxic sprays to kill off everything just so they can get their produce to the market. They are stripping the soil of its health, and are raising nutritionally dead produce. The farmers' own existence requires them to "screw thy neighbor" (that's you!) with poisons and toxins in the food supply, just so they can survive another day. The swinging low prices of food at the commercial dock can be so low that the farmer can't actually afford to pay his employees to pull the produce out of the ground. Case in point:

I have seen onions in Panama priced at $80 per 100 lb. bag. Our local farmers have had fields of onions ready to go to the market in a few weeks, and the $80 price will give them enough money to pay the bills and maybe pay down a loan. But just before their onions are ready, many government authorized containers of cheap, internationally liquidated onions hit the docks in Panama, and the huge bloated supply of onions drives the price down to $15 per bag. At this price, the local farmer can't afford to pay his help to go get the onions out of the field. The onions will now rot in the field and months of love, investment, care and attention will be destroyed, then plowed under for another crop to be planted. A few things happened here:

1. Someone internationally dumped an over-supply of onions into the Panama market at a barn burner price.

2. Someone at the government level authorized this import and knowingly or unknowingly destroyed their local farmers in doing so. What was the financial or power benefit for government agents to allow this import while destroying their own people? This is commonly known as high treason against the people of that nation, as well as treason against the national food security of a country.

3. Local farmers lost a huge investment in time, money, and massive crop risk. They will need to try to recover somehow with no government help. They will go into survival mode to feed their family, their farms and their workers.

4. Anything can happen when small farmers get desperate. Douse the food with cheaper, more harmful sprays. Screw someone in the distribution chain, and adopt "Screw them before they screw you" attitude. Become selfish and unwilling to give and be equitable, which can result in harsh treatment towards neighbors, employees, spouses and children. Screw the employee however possible to save a few dollars. Poverty and injustice is a horrible task master to the adult human soul.

5. The end user retail client probably will not see a benefit in a reduced onion price. The grocery store chain doesn't offer the discount to their clients. Restaurants don't lower their prices because of cheap onions. The profits are all absorbed and enjoyed at the

distributor/middle man level. And this, all at the expense of the local farmer who was planning to keep us supplied and fed. This farmer is the beginning of our food supply chain, and he is being destroyed daily, weekly, monthly and yearly. When will this stop? It won't without a Global Food Revolution.

6. The farmer had no idea that this hurricane level event was coming. Had he known, he could have taken some sort of evasive action. But the storm came suddenly. It wasn't a natural storm, but a storm at a man made, corporate and government level that laid his fields to waste.

Just recently Panama farmers, including me, stopped growing peppers because another national company was flooding the market with cheap peppers through their unsustainable, money losing farming model. When this company stopped producing peppers to change out their plants for a new crop, the price of peppers sky rocketed. Why? No one was growing peppers because it was a money losing crop. Peppers had been low, between $0.40 - $0.60 cents, though it costs a farmer $0.70 cents to break even. When farmers stopped growing because they couldn't afford the sustained losses any longer, there were no peppers on the market when the big corporate company stopped producing. Pepper prices shot to the moon at $1.50 - $1.60 per pound. When the little farmers saw this new price they started planting peppers in hopes of getting in on this wonderful new price. But by the time their peppers were ready to harvest, the big company was ready to flood the market again. Coupling that with fresh imported liquidation peppers and the price dropped down to horribly low prices of $0.08 per pound! The local farmers were decimated once again and lost everything! It cost more to fill the gas tanks to get their trucks back to the

51

farm, than what they made selling a truck load of precious peppers at the wholesale market that month! What a tragedy. Their government failed to protect them and give them warning of pending pepper crisis that was on the horizon.

Another case in point:
A good friend of mine consults local lobster fishermen in British Columbia. They are enslaved to a corporate system that strips them of their dignity every year as they try to perform their tasks as fishermen for their community.

These fishermen must repair the fishing vessels, mend and replace the nets, and prepare for a big fishing season on the open seas. In order to do this, they must get credit from the supply companies with hopes of making enough money during fishing season so they can pay off the loans and have something left over to feed their families.

Once they gather a fishing harvest, whether large or small, they transport their catch to the docks and are told that the prices are deflated this year. Unfortunately, they will not be able to get enough per pound of fish to pay off the loans and make money for the family. They will have worked an entire year for nothing. This happens again and again, year after year. Once in a while they are extended enough extra cash per pound to feel like they can recover. Enough hope is extended to make them fish for another year. But the deflated prices of their catch keep them in slavery to their investments, their boats and their fishing careers. "Maybe next year will be the big year," they say, hoping to pay off the ever increasing loans and interest on their fishing business.

What if I told you that the companies who dictated the prices of the lobster and fish at the dock were the same companies who own the supply businesses who offer credit to the fishermen? What if you found out that the price at the dock is potentially built to keep the fisherman in slavery to their system? What if the whole industry were set to keep private business fishermen in total slavery and captivity to the system, unable to get out because of mounting debt and loans? What if the only way out of debt for the fisherman was either death, or to quit and file bankruptcy?

And furthermore, what if many different food industries around the world are set up the same way, keeping the small producer enslaved to a larger corporate conglomerate system of greed, slavery and mass control? Would you be willing to call for a Global Food Revolution, and demand freedom for your local food providers? It's time for a full on Global Food Revolution! And it's time for governments, industries and their employees, board members, owners and investors to call out this evil, immoral corporate greed wherever it's found! Activism is necessary.

Wikipedia says that activism consists of efforts to promote, impede, or direct social, political, economic, or environmental reform or stasis with the desire to make improvements in society.

Fortunately, the United Nations is calling for this revolution as well. We finally have some backing at top international levels, where they see the need to dismantle these old unsustainable systems.

I know of a company in one nation which set up a huge facility to export their produce into another nation. They got special tax credits and discounts to build their facility because their promise was to NOT sell produce into their own country, but to provide jobs and help their national economy through export. But after running a failed business model for a period of time, they lost some of their export contracts and could not maintain profitability. Therefore, they began to quietly thrust massive amounts of their produce into a small national market, sinking the price of that produce to continual, all-time lows. This was done with government permission at high levels. All of the little farmers who were previously able to pay their bills would now be the ones paying the ultimate price for this monstrous concession to big business. They will continually pay by the pound of produce forever, because this large company was allowed by government officials to modify their business plan to the great harm of the small local farmer. Their failed business plan would be bailed out by the local farmers forever into the future with lower prices in which the local farmer cannot compete. This was, in my opinion, either corruption or inept decision making policy by that country's government to allow such a modification to be thrust on the backs of the local farmer.

The little farmer has been bailing out unsustainable corporate business models for decades, and it's getting worse. But who will bail out the local farmer? As of now, no one! It's time to join the Global Food Revolution and break this nightmare off of the backs of our beloved little farmers!

At this time the local farmer must figure a way to produce the same produce as the big corporate farms with less nutrition, less cost and in less time. The result will be product with much less nutrition and a red level spray that kills everything from insects to fungus and bacteria. "Hose it down boys! We have a farm to save!"

These scenarios happen all the time. They're immoral and they are flat out wrong! Where is the love, care and protection for our most prized small farmers? They do what they do as a calling and certainly not as a cash cow. They are upside down in their investments and business models. They are enslaved to an antiquated, immoral and unsustainable system. But somehow they keep on going forward. If you ever wanted to meet the living words "resolve in action", say hello to a small farmer in your area. You probably have no idea what they go through on a daily basis just to survive and keep their heads above water. I challenge you to go find a local farmer at a farmer's market and ask them about what I am saying? Ask them if it's true that they are fighting to survive. And ask them if you could sponsor them, support them and help in any way possible. Watch their reaction as they hear someone who is asking all the right questions and someone who actually cares.

A Global Food Revolution is needed before this unsustainable, frail system breaks in half. U.N. agencies are demanding that the small farmer makes 100% more than they currently make. (Jokingly and sarcastically I say that's $0, because 2 times $0 is still $0.) They are demanding that small farming systems become sustainable. They are mandating increased investment in food growing systems, but who would invest into this mess? They are dictating and end to inept or corrupt government oversight of the small farmer through trade restrictions and distortions which happen every day globally. They are in essence, demanding that we adopt measures that allow sustainable food commodity markets to function properly. I hope that such goals are accomplished quickly. It would restore hope and morality to bankrupt, global small farmers.

This Global Food Revolution will require mass change and overhaul at government levels, corporate levels, and at the personal/home level. We must start supporting our local farmer. We must be willing to understand sustainability and to take pride in fresh, clean, healthy foods that are not drenched in harmful chemicals and toxins. We must be willing to pay the price of recovery to help restore our local farmers. We must give them hope by supporting them locally. With compassion and passion, we must direct our time, attention and finances towards the local farmer who is ready to feed our families if given the chance. We must hold our governments to accountability, and we must stand up for and support the local farmers when they are pressed up against the wall of unsustainable debt and collapse. It's our moral duty. It's the high ground. And it's revolutionary. It's a big part of the Global Food Revolution!

Find your local farmers and support them. Buy their foods. Tell them what you are looking for and support them if they can provide it. It will boost their confidence. Go to your local farmer's markets and take your cash. Give them extra if you have it. We must help to restore and recover them from decades of corruption, slavery and destruction. We can do it, but we must ACT! Don't take this lightly or we will all pay a dear price for it in the future.

The following chapters of this book will help you to advance and prosper the Global Food Revolution in your area. Let's get started!

Key Points:

- *Many governments and corporations have united for profitability's sake to the unfortunate demise of the small local farmer. Such actions are unsustainable and immoral and must be confronted. Revolutionary thinking is a necessity.*

- *A concerted demand for the release of local farmers from the captivity of the powerful is a priority for adherents of the Global Food Revolution.*

"We know that a peaceful world cannot long exist, one-third rich and two-thirds hungry." Jimmy Carter

----

Chapter 5

You Can Join the Global Food Revolution!

"If you can't feed a hundred people, then feed just one." Mother Teresa

According to the State of Food Security and Nutrition Report 2018, the number of undernourished people in the world has been on the rise since 2014, reaching an estimated 821 million in 2017.

If you will listen carefully, you will hear them calling you. Who, you might ask? Those who cannot speak for themselves. The innocent ones that aren't old enough yet to provide for themselves. The poor, elderly, infirm and bed ridden persons who need help and care. Even governments, industries, poverty stricken nations and entire people groups are calling out for help. Their food and water supplies are diminishing. Moms are watching their babies waste away with no foreseen help on the horizon. Millions are dying right now of needless starvation with millions more to die in the future. Others have faced sudden destruction from hurricanes, earthquakes, tsunamis, cyclones, tornadoes and sudden heat/freeze of their farmlands. Their cries, pain and suffering are calling out to you and me. They are begging us to bring love, relief, care and action to their critical situations. This is one reason why we have joined the Global Food Revolution.

When you were young, did you ever hear your mother say something like, "Eat all of the food on your plate. There are children starving overseas who would love to have that food." I remember that common theme back in my day. My friends and I had heard of starving people on the other side of the world, but we always seemed to have bountiful food at home and we just didn't know anyone who was starving, or where those people were located. There was a real disconnect between people like me and those who were actually starving to death on the other side of the world, and who would love to have the food left on my plate at the end of a meal. I remember thinking, "How would we get this left over food over to those people anyway?" The only starving people I saw were on the television once in a while when a world help organization was advertising the need for help. But it just seemed so far away, too far for me to really be able to help.

As the world has gotten smaller through communications, technology and the ability to share information globally in seconds, we can now get a live glimpse of real food shortages in various nations of the world. These people are not such a great distance away any longer. And if we look closely, some of those suffering people may actually be in our own neighborhoods, communities or nations.

If you look online, you can probably find the statistics for your nation. If you happen to live in the USA which is represented as one of the most prosperous nations in the world, you will find these following statistics, as published by Why Hunger Dot Org:

HUNGER IN AMERICA (Food Insecurity)
40 million Americans are food insecure*, meaning they are often forced to skip meals, eat less at meals, buy cheap non-nutritious food and/or feed their children but not themselves.

Over 12 million children in the US are food insecure.

There are 15 million U.S. households suffering from food insecurity, or 11.8% of all U.S. households.

5.8 million U.S. households suffer from severe food insecurity, which means the people who live in them are often hungry.
2.9 million households with children are food insecure at some time each year.

40.6 million Americans currently rely on SNAP (Supplemental Assistance Program, formerly food stamps) to meet their food needs.

92% of SNAP households have incomes below the poverty line. Additionally, 82% of all SNAP benefits go to the most vulnerable households, those with children, elderly or disabled people.

Among SNAP households with children, more than half of adults work while receiving SNAP, and almost 90% are employed the prior or subsequent year. SNAP helps Americans return to work, and increasingly, it helps those who already work, but do not receive a sufficient wage to feed themselves or their families.

Many families suffering from hunger and poverty live in areas where fresh, unprocessed, healthy food is not available or is expensive, while the food they do have access to is nutritionally deficient.

The USDA defines 'food insecurity' as "the limited or uncertain availability of nutritionally adequate and safe foods or limited or uncertain ability to acquire acceptable foods." Characteristics of households with food insecurity include skipping or reducing the size of meals, not being able to afford a balanced meal, going whole days without eating, and going without food despite feeling hungry. Households with very low food security are characterized as having food intake reduced and eating patterns disrupted, because the household lacks money and other resources for food. For these households, 96% report skipping and reducing meals because of not having enough money for food.

———

"Pay attention to the hungry, both in this country and around the world. Pay attention to the poor. Pay attention to our responsibilities for world peace. We are our brother's keeper..." George McGovern

———

In 2017 the Food Security Information Network said that 1 in 9 people globally experience chronic hunger. That's 821 million people. The report says that 100 million children in developing countries are underweight. That's 1 out of 6 children. And 1 in 4 of the world's children are stunted due to malnutrition.

The 2017 report also indicated that 108 million people in 48 countries are critically food insecure, needing immediate emergency assistance.

But in 2018, the new upgraded report indicates that 124 million people in 52 countries are food insecure, a rise of 11% from the past year.

Carlos Vargas with *Hope of Life* in Zacapa Guatemala is doing a remarkable job reaching the most at risk children and others in his nation. His outreaches include his five story, free, high tech hospital to his orphan and elderly care centers, family nutritional counseling center and housing, he uses local fresh produce farming to raise nutritionally sound super foods for his operations. His operation is certainly a prototype model for the nations. Carlos is decades ahead of many in vision and reality. You can find Carlos at www.hopeoflifeministries.org; his ministry is the Hope of Life/Esperanza de Vida.

Leonard and Dagmar Weston have created the ultimate community help prototype in Piet Retief, South Africa where their influence has reached into orphanages and orphan care, public and private schooling and training of government social workers. These workers reach deep into the Zulu tribes and villages to locate and help suffering orphans who were previously lost between the cracks of failed, impoverished, tribal communities after the deaths of their parents. Weston's group works with prisoners before they are released, they assist the extreme poor to receive the medical care they need, and they provide food, medicines and school supplies to countless children in their zone. What they do is an absolute miracle and their work should be modeled around the globe. Leonard has had a powerful saying. "If your organization left town today, would your town know that you were gone tomorrow?" In the case of Piet Retief, if Wellspring Ministries left town today, many parts of the town would socially collapse into mass poverty tomorrow. What a difference they are making in their area! This is a prototype for the nations. You can find the Weston family and their prototype organization at www.wellspring.co.za . I interviewed Leonard and his staff members a few years ago and the video is located on YouTube.

Note: While the work continues onward, our friend Leonard passed away just a while ago, leaving a huge deficit in the community. However, Leonard and Dagmar had trained up good leaders who continue the ministry in full force today.

Kevin and Helen Ward are in Swaziland with an extraordinary prototype organization. He is highly connected with the business and banking sectors of Swaziland as well as with the King of Swazi. After decades of faithfulness of caring for AIDS/HIV orphans and those suffering from drug and alcohol addiction, the King of Swaziland literally gave him a small abandoned mining town called Bulembu. I have seen Kevin's operation many times as well as the revitalized town of Bulembu. This town now has hundreds of orphans being cared for, multiple businesses that support the community infrastructure such as a hotel, tree/lumber milling, bakery, honey distribution center, milk production and many more businesses arising each year. This nutritionally secure town shows that anyone can do it if they follow the proper principles of community revitalization. In Bulembu, old abandoned houses are now revitalized and livable with business people and orphan care families living successfully in this wonderful community. While Swaziland is dying as a leading AIDS/HIV nation, Bulembu is thriving it and promises to be the town that saves Swaziland from complete national mortality as their prototype thrives and grows annually. Check out Kevin and Helen Ward and their incredible work at www.bulembu.org or cmswazi.org .

I spend a part of my life reaching out to hungry children. My wakeup call came one day as a young man around 21 years old. I was traveling and doing speaking engagements in public schools and addressing drug and alcohol abuse. I somehow landed south of the Mexico border one week.

There I found a community of children who were living in a dump and sitting on dirt/mud floors. Their sleeping quarters were lean-to cardboard homes. They were dirty, extremely poor, and they would eat anything out of the dump because they were so hungry. This blew me away. "How can this be?" I asked myself. "Are these the children that my mother talked about, who would love to have my dinner scraps? Yes, they were."

I couldn't sleep well for a long time after that wake up call. Over the years I began developing inside of myself, a plan that would give a portion of everything I did in my life towards children who were in "at risk" conditions. Decades later, I am still working hard to develop feeding and food growing programs, as well as farm training programs for indigent people groups. My focus is on developing nations and community leaders who realize the importance of caring for their poor, their widows and orphans within their communities. This is my drive and passion. You will find me working to help the poor and needy, developing new ways to secure nutritional super foods, clean water and medical care to those who are most "at risk". I need your help. Won't you join me? They're calling for you. Let's make the Global Food Revolution a reality for them too.

Key Points:

- *Millions are dying worldwide due to the lack of food, sudden destruction and tragedy. This is affecting the poor, elderly, infirmed, bedridden, orphans and widows to name a few.*

- *The world has become smaller and more accessible through technology and communications. Therefore, the pain and hunger of those near and far can be heard by those of us who are listening. Is that You?*

- *A concerted demand for the release of local farmers from the captivity of the powerful is a priority for adherents of the Global Food Revolution. Will you join, willingly?*

- *Contemporary examples of outreaches exist in our time reaching many, which provides non-traditional ways to promote the Global Food Revolution.*

———

"Most of our citizenry believes that hunger only affects people who are lazy or people who are just looking for a handout, people who don't want to work, but, sadly, that is not true. Over one-third of our hungry people are innocent children who are members of households that simply cannot provide enough food or proper nutrition. And to think of the elderly suffering from malnutrition is just too hard for most of us. Unlike Third World nations, in our country the problem is not having too little – it is about not caring enough! Write your elected representatives and promote support for the hungry." Erin Brokovich

———

Chapter 6

Various Ways to Address the Food Crisis

"My motto in life is 'If you think it, you can do it' and if we all apply that thought we can end hunger the world over." Dionne Warwick

---

The current and upcoming global food crisis needs to be addressed on many different levels. You may find yourself able to seize one or more of these immediately:

*Grass roots level on a "home by home" basis: every person and family member must be educated about the global food crisis that's here and growing. Proper education along with empowerment will help a person to have a sense of ownership in averting the crisis at your home level, rather than just expecting governments and corporate farming to take care of the problem. Each person needs to learn about smart and healthy food choices, how to actively put their money and influence into personal education, local farmers and food markets to help fund the revolution. Everyone must learn how to cut waste and extend the storage life of food. Additionally, it's imperative for people to learn how to grow all of their salad vegetables in a small corner of their apartment living room, on the back porch of their home, in a little greenhouse or even in their basement using new available technologies and artificial lighting if needed.

*Small commercial level basis: using high tech farming, greenhouses and new technologies allow a person to grow huge amounts of food for themselves and their communities, for profit and for humanitarian purposes.

Some people have the proverbial "green thumb" with agriculture. It is inherent for many people to grow food, to garden and to spend time with their hands in the dirt. In the past, many have had a small garden or some growing pots on the back balcony. But because of the Global Food Revolution, many people are sensing the higher call to expand their growing capacity and start growing food not only for themselves, but for others. Many are considering a larger back yard greenhouse that could easily grow all the vegetables needed for 15 – 20 families in the neighborhood. Others are considering getting into a small farming style business or community farm that will help fulfill an internal longing to garden. This will help to provide fresh foods and possibly an income of some kind to help cover ongoing monthly expenses. Still others are wanting to dive into a high tech growing environment by converting a 40' shipping container into a hydroponic lettuce farm that pushes out 10,000 heads of fresh lettuce per year. If a person lives in a home with a garage, he or she could potentially convert that garage into an LED lit accelerated farm of the future, thereby growing enough healthy food for their entire neighborhood. Likely, with a relatively small investment one could build a greenhouse in the back yard which can provide food year around for multiple families. People are happy to buy fresh local produce that's grown healthy and as organically as possible. And the poor of the area are always happy to receive any extras that the venture may produce. There's always plenty of extra food around when a person becomes actively invested and takes an interest in growing.

*Public organization, nonprofit, school and civic level basis: by providing education and tools necessary to help students, teachers and volunteers produce food to meet local demands.

Have you ever seen a school train a class of students how to erect a greenhouse and grow food for the community? Something typically happens within a student when they have an opportunity to grow food from scratch. Many times they are bitten by the "Global Food Revolution bug". They might not realize fully what has been placed inside of them at the time, but the "seeds to impact others" are planted to help change their world in the future.

We can help schools, nonprofits and public organizations to join the revolution by educating their people in various food growing programs. Education and tools are normally needed. The passion and drive for change are typically found in educational professionals and organizational leaders. And once these educators are activated, the change can be sustainable and will affect entire communities for generations to come.

Another thing that can help your community is for you to search out and find grants for your community, whether through government programs, foundations, societies or wealthy individuals who want to change their world. Most people don't have the time or capacity to search out these funding programs. But if you have the tenacity to get out there and find these funds, it could revolutionize your community to tap into the means to educate and build.

*Industry level basis: by empowering and providing education and vision to the farmer, the transportation company, processing and distribution companies to expand and increase their capacities to meet growing demands.

The fact is with huge changes coming to our world, companies will need to change, be expanded, and new companies started in order to transition into the future. Many companies and industries will need to move geographically to best meet demands. Indeed, some large companies in the USA are already moving out of cold climate zones as reported in chapter 3. Whereas others are repositioning for what they know is coming. Farms will inevitably move to better and more productive climates and logistics zones. New technologies will be sold around the world that will change the landscape of current agriculture and food distribution. If you have an entrepreneurial spirit, you are probably already seeing great opportunity to seize upon a growing global demand. You can discern a technology and industrial wave building that you can ride into the future while helping mankind at the same time, developing and expanding the food industry. What will it take to double the world's food supply in ten to twenty years? That's the magnitude of the industrial revolution wave that must hit our world.

Grab your "food grade" industrial surf board. Let's ride this "Big Kahuna" wave all the way in to shore.

*Commercial educational level basis: by empowering and providing vision to the farmer, the transportation company, and all aspects of the food growing distribution chain.

If you are employed at the commercial level or you have a relationship with farmers and food handlers, then you can activate the Global Food

Revolution among these powerful forces. At the commercial level you can gather employees and executives together to conquer community, regional or national food needs. Maybe your group can fund the building of a greenhouse for the high school down the street, providing the tools needed for educators to instill revolutionary level knowledge into the students. Find a civic or nonprofit organization and help them raise awareness or increase their capacity to find food and donate it more effectively to the needy. Empower farmers with relationship and new technologies to grow more for less. Instill into those at the commercial level that we need a united front to increase our food growing, transportation, education and technology capacities to meet current and future demands.

*Government level basis: to provide proper trajectories to governments to help meet the demands and needs of their own populations, directing precious resources to programs that will make the most sustainable impact for their people.

The fact is that governments don't have very many answers. They need education and experts in the field to bring viable options so they can help their people and provide assistance towards alleviating pending crisis in their localities or nations. You can help your government to be educated and informed, and to make the necessary moves needed when the time comes. If you have access to governmental authority, and if you have a passion to help many people rather than a few, consider utilizing your influence and education to serve your community. Your government needs your help and wisdom.

Which of these levels are you able to function within? While this book will encourage and empower you on your level, it's important that you embrace all of these levels going forward. Why? Because you are hopefully going to replicate the educational information in this book to expand the Global Food Revolution into your family, friendships, neighborhood, community and professional relational base. And as you begin this journey, doors will open for you to educate others well beyond your normal scope of influence. You will educate your family, friends, community, region, nation and possibly other nations. You may stand before policy makers, bankers, governors, kings and presidents. Governments, businesses, investment groups and educators are all searching for people like you because they desperately realize that they need a Global Food Revolution of their own. Don't worry if you're not a polished speaker. Your actions will speak louder than words, and people will come find you in order to learn what you are doing and receive some sort of education from you. This is the time and season. You can ride the wave of revolution!

Key Points:

- *This food shortage dilemma demands multi-tiered solutions ranging from grass roots to commercial and governmental levels. It will require the involvement of public and non-profit organizations, schools and civic institutions.*

- *It is critical for everyone to locate the sphere of their most effective influence, even beyond our comfort zones for this to work effectively in the Global Food Revolution!*

―――――

"I went to bed hungry many nights as a child. It was a Dream that dressed me up when I was ragged, and it was a Dream that filled me up when I was hungry. Now it's my Dream to see that no child in this world ever goes hungry, certainly not here in America, the most bountiful country in the world. We can do better...we must!   - Dolly Parton

―――――

Chapter 7

Returning to the Local Production Strategy

One way to combat world hunger is by returning to the local empowerment & production strategy.

According to a report from the Worldwatch Institute, a key to alleviating world hunger, poverty and combating climate change may lie in fresh, small-scale approaches to agriculture. The US-based institute's annual State of the World report, published January 2011, speaks about moving away from larger industrial agriculture and talks about more small scale initiatives on local levels which could relieve poverty and hunger, and help in an environmentally sustainable way. (The Guardian Story: January, 2011)

I have a question: Could education which champions food self-sufficiency and waste reduction among both wealthy and poor nations alike be more effective than increasing actual food production on a commercial scale? Yes, absolutely! As a matter of fact, if the individual is not trained in various levels of food choices, waste reduction and personal food growing options, no amount of expanded commercial production will meet the demands. We must produce more, but we must also plug the holes in the system with the 'end user'.

Worldwatch Institute goes on further to say, "If we shift just some of our attention away from production to consumption issues and reducing food waste, we might actually get quite a big bang for our buck, because that ground has been neglected," said Brian Halweil, co-director of the project. "The majority of incentives that governments give to farmers are still tied to the production mindset. The farmers are rewarded for sheer production quantity, with very little guidance for the quality they produce and the impact of their farming practices on the environment and on human health and nutrition ... It is necessary to change these incentives," he said. The projects explored in the report include community-based initiatives in urban farming, school gardening, feeding programs, and indigenous livestock preservation.

It makes total sense to attack this global food crisis at these levels. Worldwatch Institute touched on government, commercial farming, rewards and incentives, community and urban farming, school and nonprofit programs. This is exactly what the Global Food Revolution is about!

SIDE NOTE: A huge percentage of food waste takes place between the farm to the end user's table. If it's not damaged at farm or distribution level, the end user may lose it through aging, rot or damage at home. A high percentage of these losses need to be reduced. Remember one of the five U.N. "Zero Hunger" agendas is eradicating 100% of food waste. This can be done through education and technology. I personally envision food dehydrators and freeze dryers built into kitchens which look like the standard microwave. Other technologies will renovate the kitchen and pantry allowing us to preserve and save fresh produce and meats. Making wise choices on food purchased will also help to reduce waste. Hopefully sky rocketing prices won't be the forceful educator that "schools" us to make wiser decisions, but proactive and noble education will allow us to get ahead of the curve and choose wisely now. Over the years we have

74

learned many ways to preserve fresh and canned foods at home. These methods have changed everything for us and has limited our throw away fresh foods by a significant amount. This educational power has helped us to greatly reduce waste at our consumer level. It will work for you too, as you take time to learn.

Key Points:

- *Local empowerment and production strategies may be more effective in combating world hunger, poverty and climate issues. These strategies include small scale, achievable projects such as community based initiatives, urban farming, school gardening and feeding programs.*

- *Preserving food through freeze drying and dehydration, while also concentrating on consumption issues and reducing overall food waste are major contributions towards alleviating food shortage going forward into the future.*

- *Common sense ideas may very well result in more nutrition available in hard hit areas.*

"One of the greatest feelings in the world is knowing that we as individuals can make a difference. Ending hunger in America is a goal that is literally within our grasp." Jeff Bridges

---

Chapter 8

New Food Growing Technologies

"Recent research shows that many children who do not have enough to eat wind up with diminished capacity to understand and learn. Children don't have to be starving for this to happen. Even mild under-nutrition – the kind most common among poor people in America – can do it."

Carl Sagan

We are living in amazing times. While farming is as old as mankind, recent technology discoveries have propelled food growing to new levels that once would seem unattainable for the home grower and commercial farmer. The "science" of growing food has allowed us to more clearly define the enemies of food growing, as well as to better understand plant life on cellular and atomic levels. We now know what makes a plant respond favorably, and how to maximize the capacity of that plant to grow its fruit. From open field commercial farming operations to growing your garden salad in your living room, we now have many new ways (and more coming) to bolster the Global Food Revolution.

While I am boasting about new technologies available in our day and age, I don't want you to forget FACT #3. Agricultural technologies have stalled at the level of ramping up food production for the masses. I strongly believe; however, that returning to local food production will bring about new advancements and technologies for communities. These advances albeit, impractical for large, corporate farming, may be effective tools locally.

Just take a trip through Youtube and look at the massive new inventions on growing foods in bountiful ways never thought of before. We live in amazing times.

I want to warn you though, that big corporate control is coming for your food supplies. There are some diabolical plans on the horizon that will wage war against your local farmer, totally altering the direction of your family's nutrition in the conceivable future. In my opinion, the big corporate technological advancements that are coming are all about gaining control of your food supply. I don't like to be controlled and I will never be enslaved. Those joining the Global Food Revolution will refuse this as well.

Currently, big corporations are preparing to grow our protein in laboratories while at the same time demanding that cattle, pork, and chicken production ceases. War is coming to your farmers and your dinner plate. Now is the time to learn and prepare for this coming turmoil. If big corporations are successful, the world will be eating protein grown in labs, vegetable proteins produced by big corps, and combinations of insect proteins grown by big agricultural corporations for your consumption. There is already a call for cows to be eliminated due to "cow farts" messing with the climate. Other insane ideologies will surface to convince people to allow big agricultural corporations to strip our nations of the ability to grow our own protein. I can hear them now, claiming, "It's time to give up farming. Let the big corporations take care of it. Just eat this manufactured meat and pay your grocery bills. We'll handle the nutritional part. As long as it tastes good, you and your family don't have a thing to worry about." Baloney!

THIS IS WAR! And this war is coming to your local farmer. Plans are in place now to destroy at least 50% of beef production by 2030, and to bankrupt cattle ranches in your nation. The chicken, the pig, the cow, the duck, goose, turkey and all other animal proteins are on the chopping block. The powers that be are coming to snatch your food choice freedoms, offering you a fake food security that will inevitably undermine, wreaking total collapse of your family's health. At the end of the day we are being led to "Soilent Green". If you don't know what that means, Google it. And also remember that you ARE what you EAT. What's in that genetically modified wafer that you're offering us?

I will say this again. A Global Food Revolution is required. This calls for strong activism and a demand for change. War against your food supply by the powers that be must be met with strong resistance and activism. War has been declared against you and your farmer. You must stand up and defeat those who are planning to control your food security. It won't be easy. And it will require a true Global Food Revolution.

Let's review just a few (not all) of the new technologies that we can benefit from and the home and community level. Knowing your current options will allow you to better choose your method(s) of growing food. The options are expanding every day with entrepreneurial innovation, science and hands on application.

AT HOME HYDROPONICS: There are many different hydroponic growing models that you can get ahold of to grow your own salads, fruits and vegetables right at home. The size of your living space doesn't matter. From garden grow towers to bucket systems, float beds and desktop grow planters, you can benefit from growing your own healthy, natural lettuce, tomatoes, peppers, onions, kale, swiss chard and more. Educate your entire family and enjoy a lot of vegetable output with very little fertilizer or water input. And imagine always having so much food around that you have to go to your neighbors to give it away. At some point, you might want to grow yourself into a micro business that supplies people with nutritious foods in your community. It's super easy, it's fun, and there's nothing like eating the fruits of your own labor!

I must say that if my neighbor was growing vegetables hydroponically in their garage, back porch or in a small greenhouse, I would absolutely support them and buy from them. I could do this, knowing that the food is clean, local and grown from someone I can trust. I believe other neighbors would have the same attitude. And if I'm growing tomatoes and you're growing lettuce, what an opportunity to trade produce between one another. What kind of community interaction could you develop with ten community families all growing in unison with one another? It's an exciting concept. Wouldn't you agree? That's a community that I would want to live in.

TURN EMPTY SPACE INTO VEGETABLE GROWING: Technologies and growing systems are available now to help you retrofit your garage, basement, attic, an extra bedroom or an outside porch into a healthy growing environment for growing fresh vegetables. With LED lighting, minimal electricity and water usage, hydroponics, aquaponics, aeroponics and more are all available at your fingertips. Think small or dream big. It's all possible now with DYI (do it yourself) systems or full packages ready to assemble and grow. Just think for a moment. Do you have some extra space available somewhere that could be an optimum growing location for your family's sustained food security?

79

Before jumping into any one system, I recommend that you watch 100 Youtube videos on the subject, learn from those who are educating and telling their story, and ask questions until you're absolutely satisfied that you have the right system for you. All of these technologies are developing at lightning speed and what was cutting edge last year could now be old tech this year.

GROWING COMMUNITIES: Sustainable growing communities are popping up all over the world as mankind is sensing a shift in food security and good people are developing new ideas. One of the most awesome food secure communities I have ever seen was in Osa Penninsula, Costa Rica back in 2013. Entrepreneur Jim Gayle had developed a sustainable food community where the roads and sidewalks were lined with vegetable plants rather than flowers. The 100+ home community was aided by a 5 acre, 5 employee farm that produced much of their fruits, vegetables and protein including fresh water shrimp and chicken. Wow! Every week the truck came to the homes and allowed them to choose what they wanted from the farming harvest. This was included as an overall package resulting in cheap, monthly Homeowners Association fees. This offered a reduced cost of living for those in the community. The community farm also produced enough food to send out extra to the poor families in other communities. And of course, the farm workers all had plenty to eat for their families. It was a "win-win" situation for many. The Osa Penninsula scenario was a fully sustainable community and a model for many more to come in the future! While Jim has moved on to other amazing sustainable food growing ventures, you can see this awesome community at www.osamountainvillageecostarica.com . And look Jim up with his new micro green super food growing systems that can easily be set up in your home town anywhere in the world. He is a ground breaker and is working to decentralize the growing of super foods down to the home and community level. If you want to learn from a real entrepreneurial food champion, find Jim Gayle and whatever his hands are on at the time. He's an amazing guy with a huge heart for humanity. I found him recently at www.mobilegreenswellness.com .

OPEN FIELD PLANTING: Open field planting is the age old form of farming and growing food. From the back yard garden to the 1,000 acre wheat field, this style of growing has many enemies. The crops are open to all forms of attack, whether wind, driving rain, hail, animals, rodents, insects, bacteria, virus, fungus, soil deficiencies, underground water and pollution. Any farmer who can keep those elements at bay long enough to bring out a substantial harvest has my utmost respect. From experience, it's not easy growing in an open field environment. Technologies are making things easier, but many times they come with a huge cost. And the big corporate, non sustainable way is to hose it all down with red level toxic chemicals that hold back the enemies long enough to get a crop out of the ground. That crop may look good, but it came at a horrible cost to the land, the nutrition within the food, and the person who will be eating that toxic embalmed food.

BACK YARD GREENHOUSE: Greenhouses are popping up all over the world, giving people the opportunity to grow food year around. The benefits of a greenhouse help reduce or eliminate 90% of the enemies of agriculture including: insects, animals, rodents, fungus, bacteria, wind, driving rain and snow, among other enemies. With 90% reduction in problems, the other 10% is very manageable year round with greatly reduced time input. Before considering a greenhouse, consider getting expert advice. Some of the things you must consider include, but are not limited to:

*What is the best place to locate your greenhouse in relation to sunlight, wind patterns, natural and man made structures around your greenhouse.

*What is the best style, design and size of your greenhouse, depending on your weather, winds, rain, hail and snow fall, and the enemies that you need to combat in your area by using the greenhouse.

*Consider developing new technology around your greenhouse based on potential weather changes that could be coming your way. One man I met in the Bahamas has an aquaponics commercial lettuce greenhouse that he "hurricane hardened" against the big storms that come through. When everything else is destroyed by a hurricane's path, he goes to work the next day and harvests beautiful organic aquaponic lettuce for his restaurant clients at top dollar. His greenhouses are hurricane hardened. How can you harden your greenhouses for potential weather pattern changes?

*Try to decide how much food and what kind of food you want to grow before determining if a greenhouse is right for you. Once the structure is up, you must then decide if you are growing in the ground, with raised beds, hydro, aqua, aero technologies, vertical farming, etc. Make sure and backwards engineer your entire operation with the end in mind first. How much food and what kind of food do you want to have in your hands? With this end goal in mind, you should be able to structure a project that will provide nutrition you desire. Make sure and consider adding to your project for mistakes, failures, a bad crop, bad seed, unforeseen weather or enemies of your harvest. They do come and they will come, even with a greenhouse over the top of the project.

COMMERCIAL GREENHOUSE: Greenhouses have been a powerful way to ward off 90% of the enemies of open field planting, as mentioned earlier. And when a plant is free from attack, it becomes much more happy and willing to direct its energies to fruitfulness. Greenhouses typically produce multiplied times more harvest than traditional open field planting. They can be cheap or expensive depending on the materials used to build them. A commercial farming operation must incorporate this capital building expense into the overall cost of production. A greenhouse also must be maintained with new plastic, materials as necessary, repairs to structure, etc. Your crops and the sale price must reflect the cost of the greenhouse if you are to stay in the business of growing food. If you have a small greenhouse as a hobby, then costs probably won't be a determining factor.

I learned about commercial greenhouse growing from a friend in Panama who is the "KING" of growing his commercial vegetables. When he was teaching me about building greenhouses and preparing for commercial farming, he told me stories of failed greenhouse operations where the owners would build expensive greenhouses with high technology that couldn't actually pay the bills. The high cost of their ideas didn't raise the price of their vegetables at the market. After telling me all of those stories of failure, he then said to me, "Do you want to gold plate your greenhouse and look good, or do you want to grow food? Make the choice before you build." I chose not to gold plate our greenhouse operation and it saved us from market devastation. I have learned to listen for wisdom and then follow it when it presents itself.

Remember that there are many different styles of greenhouses. Choose the one that best suits your climate, altitude, wind and rain levels and other factors. Every dimension of that greenhouse must be considered before constructing it in your area. To make a mistake and build the wrong greenhouse, or to position it improperly on your land, could potentially be very expensive, and possibly disastrous to your agriculture business. With informed and proper forethought, these problems can be avoided.

HYDROPONICS: This has been one of the buzz words of commercial food production in recent history because of its powerful capacity to grow foods quickly, scientifically and naturally without pesticides, fungicides and bactericides. Typically, the food grower provides a water solution with a suitable mix of plant foods and micro nutrients at a perfectly prescribed PH level in the water. This makes a happy plant while accelerating growth and fruitfulness. While hydroponics is not true organic farming (simply because the definition of organics do not allow hydro inclusion), hydroponic production is a super healthy and nutritional way to grow food for the future. I have seen hydroponic companies take a lettuce seed and bring it to a full, huge head of lettuce in less than 28 days. I have heard that others are doing it even quicker with 24 hour grow lights and other technological breakthroughs. This is an amazingly new scientific way of growing foods outside of soil substrate.

You will see the word "hydroponic" in many of the grocery stores today, indicating that the food represented is more likely than not, very healthy and free from a lot of harsh chemicals.

Hydroponics is being used to grow so many vegetables in commercial facilities as well as in home growing units. You can build your own DYI

84

or buy a pre-fabricated unit for your application. You can use systems that return the water to be reused over and over (reducing water usage by up to 90%) or send it to the plant through a one time application, allowing the water to escape after the plant has benefitted. People grow hydroponically in PVC pipes, rock and lava substrates, float beds, flood and drain systems, and a variety of other ways. By the time you've read this book there will have been many more ways discovered to grow hydroponic produce. However, the principle is the same and the food is delicious and healthy.

AQUAPONICS: This powerful growing strategy is "up and coming" but has had a few commercial drawbacks which I will discuss in a moment. Fortunately for the home user, I have seen countless systems in operation that simply work. And the owners of aquaponics not only enjoy fresh organic vegetables, but they are also growing protein (fish) concurrently with no additional input.

Aquaponics is about the same as hydroponics, except it's considered true organic, and delivers a new type of food into the growing system. Aquaponics uses fish tanks to produce the food that the plants will need to grow a harvest. This food is the waste from fish excrement, which the plants love to eat. Thereafter, the plants will add oxygen to the water to feed the fish in a complete closed loop cycle of plant and protein production.

A good explanation of aquaponics is this: the combination of aquaculture (raising fish) and hydroponics (the soil-less growing of plants) that grows fish and plants together in one closed loop, integrated system. The fish waste provides an organic food source for the plants, and the plants naturally filter the water for the fish. Microbes (nitrifying bacteria) are also included.

These bacteria convert ammonia from the fish waste first into nitrites, and then into nitrates. Nitrates are the form of nitrogen that plants can uptake and use to grow. Solid fish waste is turned into vermin-compost that also acts as food for the plants.

People around the world are connecting aquaculture and hydroponics with impressive results on a smaller scale. I have seen these systems in operation and they seem so simple. Yet there is an element of control and science that you must use to keep everything alive and healthy. If you allow certain water, PH, nitrate levels to go too far outside of the boundary lines, you could lose your fish, your plants, or both. But just imagine the fish feeding the plants and the plants making the fish healthy and happy. Your input typically is fish food and oxygenating the water. The output is not only organic level food production, but also fish as protein for your diet. Awesome!

On a commercial level, I have personally seen systems that struggled to make a profit, the larger their systems became. Once the system gets too large, it's harder to maintain the proper levels for the closed loop system. I interviewed an aquaponics commercial company in Missouri USA a few years ago and they said that after multiple years of operation, they were "almost" profitable. This concerned me personally because they are professionals at this, and I am a novice. If they were having troubles with commercial level aquaponics production, then I would be way behind their capacity if I tried the same commercially. However, I have since heard of different aquaponics operators who are commercially profitable and sustainable.

A small home or community aquaponics system seems to be very manageable and sustainable with much less risk involved. If a large commercial facility loses its fish and plants, it could take 90 days to regrow and hundreds of thousands of dollars of loss. If a small system loses its fish and plants, it could take 90 days to regrow and a couple hundred dollars. Manage risk well. Small aquaponics systems are a great way to manage risk of loss.

There is a great U.S. based non profit company that is sustainable. They offer to train people how to do the same. But in order to go to their training, you will have to go to "Growing Power" in Milwaukee, WI where you can freeze boiling water by throwing it in the air during winter months. Yet they use the heat from composting to heat their greenhouses and they grow year around. They boast of one million pounds of food on three acres of land including tilapia and yellow perch production. Check them out at www.growingpower.com .

Indeed science is getting better and groups like Growing Power are finding new ways to overcome the enemies of the aquaponics growing ideology. Aquaponics is a viable way today for local food production, and in the near future I'm sure it will be flourishing globally in the commercial world.

WAREHOUSE HYDROPONICS/AEROPONICS: Imagine a world where the plants are stacked high, totally enclosed in a controlled environment of conditioned air and 24/7 LED lighting, and fed exactly what the plants need for mass production? This technology is a booming way to grow food in urban areas close to the consumer and their grocery stores. There are many of these facilities popping up, but let's look at just one of them in Chicago, Illinois of all places. Chicago hasn't been known in the past as an agriculture industry. But that could change when companies like Green Sense Farms come to town.

Green Sense Farms built a pair of huge climate-controlled grow rooms in its Chicago-area production warehouse. By combining towering racks of vertical hydroponic systems with Philips new "light recipe" LED grow lights, Green Sense Farms is able to harvest its crops 26 times a year. They use 85 percent less energy, 1/10th the amount of water, no pesticides or herbicides, and reducing the facility's CO_2 output by two tons a month. Their system even produces an average of 46 pounds of oxygen *every day*. It produces little waste, no agricultural runoff and minimal greenhouse gasses because the food is grown where it is consumed.

Other commercial growing groups are using aeroponics which is close to hydroponics. Rather than the roots living in circulating water, the roots are given a mist of nutrient rich water, allowing them to breath oxygen. This helps maintain the plant's health and keeps the roots free from disease and other problems when always submerged in water. Look up "Chicago's Huge Vertical Farm" and be amazed with the results.

With mass food crisis coming worldwide, imagine growing garden-fresh foods in a restored warehouse with a completely controlled climate. It doesn't matter if the sun is shining, the wind is blowing or the rain is falling. Total controlled atmosphere gives a sort of "Garden of Eden" environment for the plants to produce and reproduce.

Every major city needs companies to invade and provide locally produced foods. You could be one of those companies who would accelerate the Global Food Revolution through high tech commercial growing techniques.

CONTAINER GREENHOUSES: Many groups are using shipping containers to house their growing systems, from hydroponic foods to mushrooms, to complete growing systems for open field farming. Check out the new "two acre farm packed in a container that doubles as a farm building" on the internet.

Also examine Stud Pac hydroponic container growing systems. They can show you the concept of growing lots of food in a small 24/7 growing environment.

Many more technologies are coming to the forefront. We are able to grow food almost anywhere. Grow it in your living room, your garage, basement, attic or on your wall. Grow it indoors or outdoors, using LED lighting or the light of the sun. I urge you to grab a technology that suits you and start growing. Do it for yourself, your family, your community and for the world which is in desperate need of food.

One great "Back to Eden" farmer shows you how to grow your soil, change rocky soil into usable farmland and use only a rake in all your farming endeavors. Paul Gautschi taught his dogs to eat whatever they wanted from the garden. This walk through education is well worth the time spent, and you learn age old truths and principles that simply work. Look up the Youtube video "Back to Eden" and "Paul Gautschi". Simply amazing.

Some of my other favorite farmers who are famous on Youtube are Gabe Brown with Cover Crops, John Kohler with Grow Your Greens, and Joel Salatin with Polyface Farm. If you get started with these great guys, you will be on the right path to choosing the food growing process that's right for you.

I also highly encourage you to watch the video called "Terra Preta Agri Char".

Curtis Stone the Urban Farmer teaches you how to grow a $100,000 per year income on ½ acre of rented farmland or urban back yards. He has books, videos, online help tools and a store where you can buy supplies and farming tools like what he uses. He has mastered the art of urban farming. He is using the power of the local farmer's market coupled with people who have joined the Global Food Revolution. Collectively, they have joined forces as individuals with a similar philosophy regarding their health, nutrition and food they enjoy, and who are also willing to pay more for their fresh local produce. He has tapped into the future of revolutionary food secure people who care.

There are many professionals who are sharing their professions, experiments and knowledge on video, blogs and web sites. Use their information. Find your most trusted professionals and subscribe to their channels and blogs. Support them. Ask questions. Learn what you can from them. Replicate what they're doing as you are able. And teach those around you how to also do what you're doing. There is a new found hunger and thirst for this type of education. This is the season to learn local food growing, and to teach it to anyone who will listen.

Key Points:

- *New food technologies present opportunities for food to be grown commercially and domestically, even within our own homes.*

- *Will You stand by while the ability to choose nutritional, fresh food is removed? A Global Food Revolution will not allow this to happen. Not on our watch!*

"The war against hunger is truly mankind's war of liberation." John F. Kennedy

----

Chapter 9

The Poor and Hungry Are Crying Out for Help

"When people were hungry, Jesus didn't say, "Now is that political, or social?" He said, "I feed you." Because the good news to a hungry person is bread." Desmond Tutu

----

You don't have to go very far to find the poor and hungry around you. If you will do a research project in your community, you will find them. Who and where are the people who are hungry, malnourished, and suffering, etc. Your city council members, mayor, governor, social service groups and local food banks should know these stats and where these people are located. Start your quest by obtaining verifiable statistics from those "in the know" before you start any feeding project for the poor. Ask these agencies what the actual needs are in your community and exactly who needs your help? Don't miss the mark by not studying the facts first. Don't launch out to help those who really don't need it. And don't provide the poor with rice if they really need chicken. Target the provable problems in your community and develop a plan to hit that target, provide sustainable, measurable change, and meet the need on a continued basis. If possible, educate your people out of their poverty while helping to meet their short term nutritional needs. Help them develop pathways to success, better jobs, greater job skills and education.

"There is no finer investment for any community than putting milk into babies." Sir Winston Churchill

Many times the poor are not able to pick themselves up. Children, widows, and the elderly are especially vulnerable as they might not have the capacity to generate income or necessary support systems to overcome their poverty. The homeless seem to be everywhere and need their own Global Food Revolution! This is when the community needs to step up to the plate and use creative designs, new ideas and a dose of volunteerism to help solve tough situations in which the poor are stuck. It's truly admirable to see community members crack the code to release the poor from malnutrition, hunger, homelessness, joblessness and hopelessness. Maybe this is something that you are being called to do, to head up, or to volunteer for when the opportunity arises. Opportunities are everywhere around us, no matter where you live. Look up as you're driving around. The need is very close at hand.

Consider developing a successful plan that can be duplicated in various communities and nations by other community volunteers. You can provide the functioning, provable prototype and allow the others to duplicate it by investing in their own communities, among their own hurting people.

I believe in prototypes. I build prototypes wherever I go. My goal is to build it once, and then replicate it all over the world by educating others how to do the same thing. You can build your own prototype project in your community and then help others to do the same.

My life's mandate is governed by the following Bible verse as the utmost authority and priority for me, which may also provide inspiration for you:

James 1:27 (NIV) [27] *Religion that God our Father accepts as pure and faultless is this: to look after orphans and widows in their distress . . .*

Key Points:

- *We will always have the poor and hungry among us, unless there is sustainable intervention.*

- *Wisdom dictates that we focus on measurable targets to succeed over time.*

- *Can You afford not to join the Global Food Revolution Now?*

———————

35 million people in the U.S. are hungry or don't know where their next meal is coming from, and 13 million of them are children. If another country were doing this to our children, we'd be at war." Jeff Bridges

———————

Chapter 10

Buy or Rent a farm and Make Your Community "Food Secure".

'My grandfather used to say that once in your life you need a doctor, a lawyer, a policeman and a preacher but every day, three times a day, you need a farmer."
Brenda Schoepp

It's possible to buy or rent farmland, and sometimes renting is better than buying. You will need to weigh the risks, legal options and short/long term objectives before buying or renting. In Panama, we can buy good farmland for $50,000 per hectare ($20,000 per acre). But there are some farmlands available for rent for $1,000 per hectare per year. In other words, I could rent a hectare of farmland for 50 years and grow the exact same amount of food on it as if I had bought that farm land for $50,000. Which would be better use of my seed money? There will be questions to ask before making an informed decision, but it's entirely possible to rent land and keep the investment at a minimum rather than to buy up front with much larger capital expense. Consider the risks, inputs and outcomes before hastily rushing to purchase of farm land.

If you can rent land in your area, consider going mobile first. Put your equipment and harvest activities into cheap used, portable shipping containers. These can be moved or sold in the future if you decide farming is not for you. Don't build anything that can't be easily moved such as a greenhouse or out building. Lease land for as long as possible with an option to exit the lease if you choose to do so in the future. Additionally, consider inserting an option to purchase the farm during the lease, in case you are ready to dive in and own that land in the middle of your lease. Being mobile and flexible on leased land can be a great way to begin farming as it's easier to stop and liquidate if it doesn't turn out the way you wanted. Imagine selling a failed farm with permanent buildings and concrete structures on that farm. Who wants to buy a failed farm? Maybe at a liquidation price, which would cost you dearly.

One must develop a thorough, strategic, farming plan before entering the farming business, especially in advance of the anticipated, worldwide food shortages across various parts of the globe. In that day, all the dynamics will change from the price of farmland, to the prices of fertilizers, seed, farm equipment and the price of food. That day is rapidly approaching but has not hit yet. Therefore, you can get into place before greater food challenges are upon us.

There are strategies that you can adopt that will cause you to make good money in farming, but you must find the secret keys to your area. This will require asking 10,000 questions and researching the food needs, demands and prices in your area.

In my opinion it will also require that you consider the greatest expenses that farmers normally incur. If you want your farm to be sustainable in a day when war has been declared against farmers, you must be able to reduce expenses, maximize production, and find a sustainable market in which to sell. Our highest expenses are employees, fertilizers and insecticides / fungicides / bactericides. We are continually learning how to think outside the box and then exiting the strategies that are too expensive to be sustainable. We are learning the age old secrets of organic, non-commercial farming techniques that totally defeat the commercial farmer's business plan. Further, one must learn these secrets also to be competitive and to offer a high quality food at a reasonable price that your clients can afford.

Starting up a farm may require massive sacrifice while you are ramping up operations. Unless you have a nest egg set aside to provide for you needs while you build, grow and learn, you may need to find alternate income when you embark on the farming venture.

The United States Department of Agriculture's Economic Research Service reports that, by far, the majority of new farmers rely on off-farm income to support themselves. This means that many new farmers need to have supplemental income to sustain themselves while building a viable and profitable farm. This information is critically important when developing your farm strategy. Why? It's entirely possible that you might need to supplement your farm income with outside funding until the time that you become profitable and self-sufficient. Don't forget to figure in "Plan B" in your overall strategy. Says who? Says the USDA!

Why do farmers need to supplement their incomes with outside sources? Because of the war that's been declared on the small farmer. Small farmers have been squeezed and squeezed until they've had to acquire other jobs in order to keep the farms. This is not sustainable in the long run. And this is why the U.N. is calling for the small farmer to increase their incomes by 100% in this next Global Food Revolution.

If your farming business plan includes a "Plan B" off-farm income as a backup, you need to look at the requirements for finding a job in your farm area, commuting to that job, and figuring the work hours vs. farming hours required in your overall farming business plan. You will need to work extra hard to make it work, and it may require a lot of extra effort in the beginning. I suggest that you get your alternative income going in advance of starting the farm project so there is no loss of supporting income for you and your family.

When looking for farmland and considering a "Plan B", you may need to narrow your search area by considering which counties have off-farm employment options, where the markets for your farm products are located, and where the necessary farm support services are located (fertilizers, equipment, employees, repairs, etc.). If it's possible to create perspective online income or to conduct an internet business while farming, then finding secondary employment in your area will not be of necessity. You may therefore move anywhere to start your farming venture, including the third world.

It's helpful to get an old-fashioned paper road map and draw two circles: one with the off-farm job locations in the center and a radius as long as the distance you are willing to commute. The other circle will include your customer base in the middle and a radius as long as the distance you're willing to travel to market. Where the circles overlap is where you should look for land.

Find and buy farmland by doing four things:

1. Be clear and realistic about the budget you'll need to support yourself and your farm, and about how you'll get the income you need.

2. Do your homework on the neighborhood and the land you're interested in, to ensure it suits you and the type of farming you want to do.

3. Think outside the box: Be open to different options and timetables for buying or renting land.

4. If you apply for a loan, find out what mortgage lenders require from borrowers and get those requirements in order.

5. Merge your data including seasons, altitudes, environment, types of foods you can grow, crop cycles, full annual budget and profit potentials, and creative options for renting or buying farmland, equipment and capital expenses (like greenhouses).

Evaluating Farmland: Even in this electronic age, plenty of rural land changes hands without being advertised. Contact a local realtor and ask around at local cafes or farm-oriented businesses to find out who might be considering selling their property.

Listed are key aspects to consider when evaluating a farmland:

- Is the water clean and sufficient for the needs of both the family and the farm?
- Is the soil farmable?

• Are the buildings, fences and utilities in working condition? If not, how much time and money will infrastructure improvements require?

Water is one of the most important requirements for farmland. You must have an abundant supply of water during your projected seasons of farming, or you are simply out of business. To have a continual redundant supply of water is a huge commercial benefit. If you have any doubts about the quality, quantity or reliability of the farm water supply, consult with a well driller or other professionals.

Soil is the next important aspect to consider. Whether land can be farmed is determined primarily by soil type, as described in the USDA and Natural Resources Conservation Service's (NRCS). Read the descriptions of the soil types, because these will help you understand what you can and cannot farm in soil. You will learn the depth of topsoil and subsoil, drainage, degree of slope, and which crops and farming activities that soil will sustain.

Side Note: *If your soil is not farmable, there are ways to grow new soil over time which will sustain viable farming. There are also options in hydroponics which require no soil at all to grow food, only using the land as a footprint to house a hydroponic food delivery system that uses no soil and requires very little water.*

Talk with a soil fertility specialist such as an extension soil expert about what bringing the soil to its full potential may cost. Also consult with people who are professionals at growing soil from rocky ground. Paul

Gauchi is one of the guys to learn from with his "Back to Eden" video on Youtube, whom I've mentioned earlier. He is most certainly out of the box!

Buildings, utilities and support services are other options to consider. If you're uncomfortable with your ability to judge the soundness of buildings and the condition of plumbing, wiring, the furnace, fences and the septic system, find someone who can inspect them for you. You may have a knowledgeable friend or relative, or your realtor or banker may know someone locally in the neighborhood.

Before making an offer on a property, check out the neighborhood. Vacation there for a week if it's not local to you, subscribe to the local papers, talk to people, drive around, and certainly boot up Google Earth and do a virtual "fly over" of the area. Secondly, visit the county offices or website for information on land use ordinances (including zoning) and any/all current land uses. Land use ordinances at both the township and county levels may either limit or protect the types of farming and marketing you can do, and they will certainly impact the types and pace of future development. Ask most of your 10,000 questions among the local residents and county offices, to get a full understanding of what you are potentially getting into.

Getting Money to Buy Farmland: There are four traditional options to investigate for borrowing money: your relatives, a landowner willing to self-finance all or part of the mortgage through a "contract for deed," the government, or a commercial lender (such as a bank). It may take a couple different lenders to make a final deal work.

Looking good to a lender is important. Because lenders are primarily interested in how likely it is they'll get their money back (with interest), your job is to demonstrate that you're a good risk. To find out what lenders are looking for, check out the Land Stewardship Project's publication" Getting a Handle on the Barriers to Financing Sustainable Agriculture".

Thinking outside the box will also be important. What if you have no money, no experience, no off-farm employment, and so no appeal for a potential lender? Get a farm internship. Go to the NSAIS website and check its national list of internships; also check regional and state sustainable agriculture organization websites for additional opportunities. World Wide Opportunities on Organic Farms offers paid and unpaid apprenticeships on farms around the world.

Enroll in classes on sustainable farming, including the business aspects. These may be available through nonprofit regional or local sustainable agriculture organizations, through state extension and universities, or through private colleges.

Get an urban location and replicate what the Urban Farmer (Curtis Stone) is doing. Learn with a small piece of land, get sustainable produce coming out of your small farm, and catalog your successes. This farming knowledge, education and skill will be valuable when convincing a lender that you can handle a larger piece of territory.

How Young Farmers Are Getting Land: Across the world, there's a wave of interest in local food, and a new generation of young farmers are trying to grow it. Many of these farmers, many of whom didn't grow up on farms, would like to stay close to cities. After all, that's where the demand for local food is located.

The problem is, that's where land is most expensive. So young farmers looking for affordable land are forced to get creative. Lindsey Lusher Shute, Executive Director of the National Young Farmer's Coalition, says that her organization conducted a survey of 1,000 farmers in 2011, and "land access came up as the No. 2 challenge for farmers who were getting started." It came in right behind not having enough financial capital. Put simply, in areas close to major cities, especially on the East and West coasts, farmers can't pay nearly as much for land as people who would build houses on it.

In fact, it's not a new problem. Several decades ago, state and local governments, as well as nonprofit organizations, began attempts to preserve farmland that was threatened by urban sprawl.

They set up programs that give farmers cash in exchange for a legally binding promise that their land can only be used for farming, forever. As a result, farmers don't have to compete against developers for that land, making the land cheaper.

Developing a small farm through the concept of the Urban Farmer (Curtis Stone), you could rent a home anywhere in the city or in an urban area, and you could farm that land attached to that home. Make sure that urban or city ordinances permit you to do so, and make sure that the landlord is agreeable to the business venture before you dig up his back yard and start planting corn or other vegetables. Landlords don't like surprises. Let them know exactly what you are thinking about before leasing and make sure that it's included in your written lease before you sign.

Creating a Farm Marketing Plan: A good marketing plan is a cornerstone of any successful farm enterprise. When planning to sell what you raise, you'll need to figure out where there are enough potential customers and how you might sell to them, whether at farmer's markets, community supported agriculture programs, wholesale markets, direct internet ordering, or door to door deliveries, etc.

The National Sustainable Agriculture Information Service (NSAIS) (mentioned above) offers a wealth of information to help you decide what to raise and how to sell it. You'll need to seek other sources to find out whether necessary support services such as veterinarians, fertilizer companies, and organic suppliers are available in your search area. Find these resources by talking with local farmers, communicating with local vendors at farmer's markets and by picking up a copy of the local agriculture magazine in the area. Check classified ads and other places that vendors are trying to reach out to you. Start communicating with them and ask their share of 10,000 questions. While their eventual goal is to sell you something, they will normally offer you information that you are seeking.

Key Points:

- *Decide to rent or buy a farm, weighing risks, legal options, short & long term objectives.*

- *A full farming business plan is crucial, especially in advance of a local food crisis.*

- *A Global Food Revolution can begin in your backyard with careful and well-informed forethought.*

"Close to a billion people – one-eighth of the world's population – still live in hunger. Each year 2 million children die through malnutrition. This is happening at a time when doctors in Britain are warning of the spread of obesity. We are eating too much while others starve." Jonathan Sacks

----

Chapter 11

Final Thoughts:

I want to challenge you to start your own local food revolution. Find your area of interest and start promoting it. Get people involved in a local educational or feeding project. Use your friendships, contacts and business network to help feed your world around you. It's commonly said that you are only five people away from anyone in the world that you need to meet. In other words, you know someone who knows someone who knows someone who can get you the people with whom you need to communicate. That's amazing! Why not go to the top and build a network of friends and connections who are on the same page and who want to start a Global Food Revolution? Think about it and start building a network of people who have the vision for revolution.

If you are an entrepreneur at heart, you might see some amazing opportunities in front of you. With full United Nations backing and governmental direction change concerning food production and sustainable development, you just might be able to ride a wave of new innovation for huge benefits, service to the world and massive profits. Put your ideas and plans in action and build a high tech business, growing organic level food in warehouses, under LED lighting, using aquaponics, hydroponics, greenhouses, and other great new technologies that are emerging. Be a front runner and leader in your community and grow, grow, grow! You can do it. Simply get started and watch the people around you draw close. There's something in the hearts of many people these days that is looking for organic, healthy, nutritious foods that are grown with new technologies and offered by people who care. Many people are looking for a Global Food Revolution and you may be the person they are looking for to lead them into it.

As a side note, some of the top technologies that I'm seeing in this season are coming out of New Zealand and Israel. Plan to take a trip and see them, visit one of their trade shows, or get online and start researching. Amazing things are happening in those nations including fully sustainable food growing systems.

There is a great need for development of dehydration companies and nonprofit organizations who can extend the shelf life of living foods and get them into key locations for consumption. As food shortages grow globally, shelf sustainable foods are going to be required for hundreds of millions of people.

Governments are beginning to pass laws like the one recently passed in France, where it is now illegal for supermarkets to throw food away. Think about this for a moment. If they are not allowed to throw it away, why doesn't someone develop a nonprofit organization that will go in and gather that food, dehydrate and package it, and give it to the poor. It's worth considering that. Just think about how much fresh foods are sold at a supermarket. And consider that they can lose up to 10% of those foods due to mismanagement, rot or damage. But if you could preserve it through dehydration or freeze drying, you would be the "hero" of the community with so much food to distribute to the poor and needy! You could be 10% of a grocery store's output – and meeting the U.N. "Zero Waste" policy for the future. Do it!

American states like Massachusetts, Vermont and Connecticut have laws on the books forbidding the throwing away of food. Rather it needs to be donated to the poor, or used to create biogas, compost or feed for animals. You can jump on this huge wave and ride it to shore. Choose your business model or nonprofit model and run!

With world food supplies diminishing and populations exploding, we are going to need a "Super Food Revolution" where a little bit goes a long way. There are many super foods out there today which are gaining great attention, but these are going to play a prime role in many nations going into the future so people can get health benefits needed for sustainable healthy living.

Just a few super foods, but certainly not inclusive, include:

Wheatgrass, spirunila, moringa, alfalfa, flax seeds & flax hull lignans, green tea, beans, lentils, peas, peanuts, olive oil, cinnamon, okra, broccoli rape, mushrooms, hemp and seaweed.   Dark leafy greens include kale, swiss chard, spinach, collard greens & turnip greens are included in the superfood list. Roots include sweet potatoes, tumeric, ginger and garlic. Fruits include blueberries, avocados, goji berries, coconuts and grapefruit. Nuts and seeds include sunflower, pumpkin, chia & hemp seeds.

Some of my favorite super foods are worth talking more about here.

Moringa: Known as the super food of the 21st century as it contains nutritional properties unlike any other plant based food. It hails 30% protein in its leaves, high levels of Vitamins A, B, C, D, E and the list goes on with how powerful moringa is to the human body. I have pages of nutritional information on the power of moringa at root, trunk, leaf, seed, pod and flower levels. Undoubtedly moringa will be a key functioning role for many nations going forward. I have said for years that we can end world hunger and help the climate by planting a couple billion moringa trees around the world. Every city, town and rural community needs to have moringa trees in their parks, schools, churches, and back yards of anyone who is willing to grow them. I teach those in third world locations to grow moringa trees in their back yards as it is a "food secure" crop for their families.

Note: Moringa can survive locations where it gets to 32 degrees with special precautions taken to protect the roots from freezing.

Flax hull lignans are hailed as one of the great superfoods of all time, flax hull lignans have the capacity to rebuild the human immune system as well as providing massive nutrition. I have personally been involved in the antidotal initial testings of flax hull lignans as we performed 3 rounds of testing on AIDS/HIV patients, cancer victims, those affected by lupus, diabetics, high cholesterol and more.

Two rounds of testing were performed in the USA and one round in South Africa and Swaziland. Amazingly with a 97% success rate, 90 days of flax hull lignans introduced into the diet brought about massive shrinkage of tumors, full restoration of an AIDS patient immune system, prostate PSA levels dropping to normal, breast and ovarian cancers dissolving. You can get the full report on this miraculous flax based product at www.aidshivawareness.org .

Malabar Spinach: This spinach is one of my personal favorites because of what we've seen on our prototype farm. A little retired lady once gave me seven malabar spinach seeds and told me that it grows like crazy in Panama where our prototype farm is located. We put the seven seeds in the ground and they exploded upwards, climbing up the eight foot tall strings that we had prepared for it. The vines produced huge leaves, some the size of tortillas which we quickly started using as healthy spinach wraps. The vines also started throwing off massive seeds which we quickly planted. Within 90 days we had a 200 foot wall of spinach growing on our farm and had harvested thousands of seeds for helping others to plant super foods in their back yards. There were so many spinach leaves that we couldn't harvest them all. This was the most powerful growth and multiplication I had ever seen which caused me to coin our popular phrase, "Super Food, Super Fast".

Malabar spinach is also called Indian Spinach, Ceylon Spinach, Basella Alba, East Indian Spinach, Vine Spinach, Climbing Spinach, Chinese Spinach, Cyclone Spinach & Alugbati. The serving size of 44 grams provides 10 calories. It is an excellent source of iron, calcium, Vitamin B9, C and A, as well as copper, phosphorus and magnesium. It's rich in protein and has great amounts of antioxidants such as lutein and beta carotene. There is so much more that malabar spinach does. Look it up and get it into your diet.

There are so many great super foods that are easy to grow, offer super nutrition to people who are in great need, and which you can personally get involved. You can grow it, develop it, dehydrate it, package it, and/or market it. Choose your plan and execute it thoroughly. People are waiting for your products!

I remember back in the 1990s when our nonprofit organization needed to help the nation of Liberia. They were approaching winter and their crops had been destroyed by an unusual crop disaster leaving millions of their people vulnerable through the winter months with no harvest and no food. We received a gracious donation from the Pines Wheatgrass Company in Lawrence, Ks. USA and shipped a semi-truck load of powerful, nutritious Wheatgrass tablets to Liberia for distribution among the poorest and most "at risk" people. Those wheatgrass tablets saved the lives of many that winter because of their super food capacity. If you want to find a leader in super food production, look no further than Pines International! I have put this enthusiastic plug in for Ron Seibold and Pines International because they have helped on many occasions to intervene in areas where devastation has occurred. They are true servants of their community domestically and internationally with huge hearts of compassion for those in need of nutritious super foods.

You can do the same to help save entire populations from adverse weather, blight, crop failure and dire weather patterns. If you have access to super food in any part of the distribution chain, you can make a huge difference in the lives of the poor. A good business plan will generate enough profits to make your company and investors very happy, and give you plenty of extra nutrition to provide for those in dire need. There's nothing like the feeling of having a distribution network in place that can help the poor when times are critical. It brings all of the work of building and growing your company to a new level of satisfaction, not to mention the lives saved because you built a structure ahead of the curve of disasters that certain people would be facing into the future.

Key Points:

- *Develop your specific area of interest with the intention of feeding others through the Global Food Revolution.*

- *There are many examples of available super foods, globally some of which may be grown at home.*

"In this country that grows more food than any other nation on this earth,

it is unthinkable that any child should go hungry." Sela Ward

----

Chapter 12

Share Your Knowledge and Grow the Revolution

"I hope someday we will be able to proclaim that we have banished hunger in the United States, and that we've been able to bring nutrition and health to the whole world." George McGovern

----

The world needs your knowledge. They need expandable and duplicable concepts and sustainable prototypes. They need you. Whatever you do to join the Global Food Revolution, make sure that you share your information through social media, blogs, vlogs, a Youtube channel, Instagram, Facebook page, a web site or the newest way to reach out to the world. Get creative and help others do what you've already done. There's power in multiplication. Imagine a village in India finding your information and putting it to use, increasing their capacity to grow food for their village. It will happen if you put your information out there! The world is hungry. We are in the middle of the information age where everyone has a smart phone and an internet connection. They are looking for you and your story. Write or video tape your story and help them to also join the "Global Food Revolution"!

I hope that this book has been informative and enlightening to you. I am available in a limited way to help you as you and others join the Global

Food Revolution in your area. Feel free to reach out to me with questions, comments or offers to join us. Come take a trip with us to an international project that needs our help. Come visit us and put your gloves on! Thank you for your time.

Key Points:

- *The world awaits sustainable creative concepts which must be shared to curb the risk of plight of others worldwide.*

- *Today's technology enables knowledge to be broadcast via social media such as blogs, vlogs, YouTube channels, Instagram, Facebook, websites and other available "voices" to even the remotest parts of the world.*

- *Go and grow! Encouraging others to be part of the Global Food Revolution.*

- End

"Close to a billion people – one-eighth of the world's population – still live in hunger. Each year 2 million children die through malnutrition. This is happening at a time when doctors in Britain are warning of the spread of obesity. We are eating too much while others starve." Jonathan Sacks

---

Come Join Us!

Dr. Daniel & Tracy Daves currently reside in Chiriqui, Panama where they have built a prototype experimental farm. They invite you to come by appointment and enjoy the farm tour experience. The farm enjoys organic and near organic growing techniques, growing "super foods, super-fast", and developing new ideas that work in the first and third worlds for accelerated food growth. Their prototype commercial size dehydration center preserves foods that would otherwise be lost to over ripeness, rot or damage. The farm is also working with various models of organic plant food creation including rabbit manure as a base of organic plant food. You can see the farm in action at www.globalfoodproviders.com or on Facebook at: Global Food Providers.

Dr. Daniel & Tracy with a bountiful harvest of Malabar spinach super food!